When Lucifer Cometh

Literature and the Sciences of Man

Peter Heller
General Editor
Vol. 7

PETER LANG
New York • Washington, D.C./Baltimore • San Francisco
Bern • Frankfurt am Main • Berlin • Vienna • Paris

Richard D. Critchfield

When Lucifer Cometh

The Autobiographical Discourse of Writers and Intellectuals Exiled During the Third Reich

PETER LANG
New York • Washington, D.C./Baltimore • San Francisco
Bern • Frankfurt am Main • Berlin • Vienna • Paris

Library of Congress Cataloging-in-Publication Data

Critchfield, Richard.
  When Lucifer cometh: the autobiographical discourse of writers and
intellectuals exiled during the Third Reich / Richard D. Critchfield.
    p.   cm. — (Literature and the sciences of man; vol. 7)
  Includes bibliographical references.
  1. Authors, German—20th century—Biography. 2. Authors, Exiled—
Germany—Biography 3. Authors, German—Foreign countries—
Biography 4. National socialism and literature. 5. Authors,
German—20th century—Political and social views. 6. Autobiography.
I. Title. II. Series.
PT405.C76   1994   830.9'920694—dc20   [B]   93-42551
ISBN 0-8204-2313-0   CIP
ISSN 1040-7928

Die Deutsche Bibliothek-CIP-Einheitsaufnahme

Critchfield, Richard D.:
When lucifer cometh: the autobiographical discourse of writers and
intellectuals exiled during the Third Reich / Richard D. Critchfield. - New
York; Washington, D.C./Baltimore; San Francisco; Bern; Frankfurt am Main;
Berlin; Vienna; Paris: Lang, 1994
  (Literature and the sciences of man; Vol. 7)
  ISBN 0-8204-2313-0
NE: GT

The paper in this book meets the guidelines for permanence and durability of
the Committee on Production Guidelines for Book Longevity of the
Council on Library Resources.

© Peter Lang Publishing, Inc., New York 1994

Printed in the United States of America.

Contents

Acknowledgments

For their support of the research of this book I am indebted to the Alexander von Humboldt-Stiftung of the Federal Republic of Germany. I would also like to express my indebtedness to Richard Brinkmann, Wulf Koepke, Helmut Kreuzer and Katharina Mommsen, whose support, advice, encouragement and criticism played an important role in the completion of this study.

For Wops and Verena

Introduction

I

Twenty years have now passed since James Olney wrote: "Surprisingly little has been written about autobiography at all and virtually nothing about its philosophical implications" (*Metaphors of the Self*, 2). The flood of critical articles and books on autobiography in the intervening years from America and Europe reveal that a great deal has been written and continues to be written on the subject. The virtual explosion of studies in autobiography, which continues unabated, is driven by a variety of factors, ranging from what Olney would later term the "anxiety about the self" ("Autobiography and the Cultural Moment," 23), to the relatively recent interest in the lives of figures which had previously not been the focal point of autobiographical research, foremost among them are women's autobiographies.

Contributions by Germanists to the renewed interest in autobiography first centered on the history of the genre and forms of autobiographical discourse in the 18th and 19th centuries. Günter Niggle's *Geschichte der deutschen Autobiographie im 18. Jahrhundert. Theoretische Grundlegung und literarische Entfaltung* and Klaus Detleff Müller's *Autobiographie und Roman. Studien zur literarischen Autobiographie der Goethezeit* were representative of such investigations. More recent studies were concerned with the autobiographical enterprise of specific periods in the 20th century, and groups engaged in the autobiographical act. Peter Sloterdijk's *Literatur und Lebenserfahrung. Autobiographien der zwanziger Jahre* comes here to mind as does Helmut Peitsch's *Deutschlands Gedächtnis an seine dunkelste Zeit. Zur Funktion der Autobiographik in den Westzonen Deutschlands und den Westsektoren von Berlin 1945-1949*. One also thinks here of Sandra Frieden's *Autobiography: Self into Form. German Autobiographical Writings of the 1970's*, Georg Bollenbeck's *Zur Theorie und*

Geschichte der frühen Arbeitererinnerungen, and Katherine Goodman's *Dis/Closures: Women's Autobiography in Germany Between
1970 and 1914*.[1]

Still, it is surprising how little has been written about the
autobiographical enterprise of the exiles. I am referring to
the exiles who fled Hitler and Nazism. To be sure, the victory
in 1933 of Lucifer—of Hitler and the flight of writers and
intellectuals into exile signaled a new and prolific period of
autobiographical writing. Yet, with few exceptions,[2] the
autobiographical writings of the exiles, which number in the
hundreds, continue to be neglected in scholarly studies. Many
were written by prominent German and Austrian intellectuals
and writers, including Alfred Döblin, Lion Feuchtwanger,
Heinrich Mann, Ludwig Marcuse, Fritz Kortner and Robert
Neumann, to name but a few.

The subject of this book is the autobiographical discourse of
exile writers and intellectuals. Many of the autobiographies
and autobiographical texts of the exiles were written during
the Third Reich and World War II, while others appeared
after the collapse of Nazi Germany. The autobiographical
enterprise of the exiles extends into our own time. Witness
Stephan Heym's *Nachruf* (1988), Hilde Spiel's *Die hellen und die
finsteren Zeiten* (1989), *Welche Welt ist meine Welt?* (1990), and
most recently Hans Sahl's *Exil im Exil* (1991). The common
thread running through their texts is that of rupture and discontinuity. In many instances the shorter forms of such
earlier texts as Ernst Toller's *Eine Jugend in Deutschland* (1933),
Martin Gumpert's *Hölle im Paradies* (1939) and Tony Sender's
Autobiographie einer deutschen Rebellin (1939), and the tendency
to present one's life up to the collapse of the Weimar Republic,
must be seen within the context of discontinuity. In brief,
many exiles were in the middle of their lives when they fled
Germany and their texts could only reconstruct part of their
life-stories.

In recreating their lives, experiences or political convictions
the exiles would draw on the full spectrum of the autobiographical repertoire, from the autobiographical act as an act of
personal self-justification to the use of autobiography as a
vehicle of political enlightenment and indoctrination. It has

been observed that the books an autobiographer is most likely to read are other autobiographies and that these will make an appearance of some kind in the work of his hand (Fleishman, 2). Certainly, no one writes autobiography who has not read or who is not reading autobiography, and the exiles, particularly the exiled intellectuals and writers were undoubtedly acquainted with the earlier masterpieces of the canon, from Augustine's *Confessions* (400) to Goethe's *Dichtung und Wahrheit* (1833). Yet the history of exile autobiography reflects not only the reception and adaptation of earlier models of the genre, say in the texts of Alfred Döblin and Heinrich Mann, but equally such contributions to the innovation of the genre as Walter Mehring's *Die verlorene Bibliothek. Autobiographie einer Kultur* (1952).

II

But what is autobiography? The term itself is relatively new in the history of literary genres, emerging only at the beginning of the 19th century. Johann Gottfried Herder is credited as its originator in Germany;[3] Robert Southey as the creator of the term in England.[4] However, critics continue to disagree on what precisely constitutes an autobiography:" Everyone knows what autobiography is, but no two observers, no matter how assured they may be, are in agreement" (Olney, 7). Definitions of autobiography abound, but there is little or no consensus. The one view that continues to resurface is the literalist or purist position. It maintains that "autobiography is a self-written biography designed and required to impart verifiable information about the historical subject" (Fleishman, 7). The literalist position forms in turn the basis for Philippe Lejeune's concept of the autobiographical pact: the tacit and delicate understanding between the autobiographer and the reader that the former's rendering of his or her life is predicated on biographical truth.[5]

For many years the critical interest in "truth" as the central value in autobiography dominated much of the discussion of the genre.[6] That preoccupation, however, has gradually, but inexorably shifted to the view and acceptance of autobiography as literature and thus as a mixture of fact and fiction. The unavoidability of fiction in the autobiographical act is regarded today as almost self-evident. Goethe himself was keenly aware of the fictions inextricably linked to self-repre-sentation as the title of his autobiography clearly reveals. The autobiographer who, because of the passage of time is inca-pable of remembering the actual facts of his life, must inter-pret the past, and in so doing navigate the often imperceptible and always tenuous line separating truth and fiction. Or as Wayne Shumaker has written: "Even if we assume the com-plete and objective accuracy of every fragmentary recollection in the mind, it remains obvious that no autobiographer is in possession of the full truth of his past....absolute truthfulness, even in matters of fact cannot be hoped for, and a truthful recreation of the whole life, precisely as it was lived, is impos-sible" (Shumaker, 36, 48). As the autobiographer remembers, shapes and structures the past, he or she often present their life-story in the most favorable light, both for their readers and for themselves. Simultaneously the subject and object of their enterprise, autobiographers easily blend fiction and truth, illusion and reality to create in many instances a less than true picture of the self. In the end, the autobiographical enterprise is contingent, above all, on memory whose highly complex layerings and selective nature can cause the autobi-ographer to recall certain events in the past, while others which he or she may wish much more to remember remain inaccessible.[7] On the other hand, the blind spots of memory can be connected to the repression of memories whose con-scious replay would be unbearable. A flawed memory, desired or undesired, plays a key role in the fictionalization of one's past and self. Like all autobiographers, the exiles were not immune to the distortion of facts, to deception and fictions and to self-glorification.[8]

As for the role of fiction in autobiography, it has come to dominate for many critics the discussion of the genre. To study autobiography today is to study the art of self-inven-tion,[9] to explore the fictions of consciousness,[10] to wrestle with the fictions of self.[11] At the same time, critics have recently asked whether autobiography is not in its death throes, a notion leading Michael Sprinker to proclaim the end of autobiography. Referring to the hero of T. Pynchon's *Gravity's Rainbow* (1973), Sprinker predicated his pronouncements on what he termed "an unsettling feature of modern culture, the gradual metamorphosis of an individual with a distinct personal identity into a sign, a cipher, an image no longer clearly and positively identifiable as this one person" ("Fictions of the Self: The End of Autobiography", 322). Roy Pascal was thinking along similar lines years earlier when he lamented the absence in modern autobiography of precisely what he valued in Rousseau's *Confessions* and Goethe's *Dichtung und Wahrheit*, namely the autobiographer's "confidence in the ultimate wholeness and integrity of the self and in the meaningfulness of its destiny" (*Design and Truth in Autobiography*, 52). Traditional theory of autobiography has from its inception in the 19th century to more recent investigations been predicated on the concept of an autobiographical self. Georg Misch, one of the early pioneers of autobiographical research, observed at the beginning of this century that autobiography has its basis in the consciousness of self, and that in a certain sense, the history of autobiography is the history of human self-awareness (*Geschichte der Autobiographie* I, 8).

The decline, if not the end, of autobiography has often been viewed among German scholars as following in the wake of Goethe's *Dichtung und Wahrheit*. Goethe's text has continually been regarded through the years as the quintessence of autobiographical evolution (Cf. Peitsch, 17-18), as an expression of a specific bourgeois consciousness, whose decline in the 19th century precipitated that of autobiography, its preferred form of self-assertion and self-revelation (Cf. Goodman, viii). Even so, Goethe's text was regarded as the classical form of autobiography in Germany, and its structure became prescriptive in the critical discourse on "true or genuine autobiography," and not only for German scholars, but also for such prominent critics of autobiography as Roy Pascal. Central to Goethe's text was a new mode of self-conception: the conception of the self as a unique and unrepeatable individuality (Weintraub, 821-848). *Dichtung und Wahrheit* presented the story of the continuous evolution of a self, particularly its

internal development, but also its interaction and interplay
with the external world. Above all, it was considered to be a
text portraying and interpreting a life in its totality. Yet, as
Elizabeth Bruss has shown, the assertion that a specific autobiography constitutes the summation and culmination of autobiographical evolution flatly contradicts the historically
dynamic aspect of generic development (Cf. E. Bruss *Autobiographical Acts*, 5-6). Generic development can be seen as
driven by, and as a function of the changing historical
consciousness of the self and of individuality (Klaus Detleff-
Müller, "Die Autobiographie der Goethezeit," 479). Moreover, any discussion of the ontology of autobiography should
include Hans Robert Jauß's concept of the shifting horizon of
expectation that governs generic recognition of a literary text
at any given time.[12]

In point of fact, autobiography is neither in decline nor is it
coming to an end.[13] What is coming to an end is the credibility of certain prescriptive definitions of autobiography, whose
strategy was to control rather than to respond to what Janet
Varner Gunn has termed "the strangeness of autobiography"
(*Autobiography: Toward a Poetics of Experience*, 11). The strategy
to control would yield such terms as Roy Pascal's "autobiography proper", whose main focus was defined as
the story of self, whereas the hallmark of the memoir and
reminiscence was seen in the recreation of the lives and
actions of others. Earlier scholarly preoccupation with questions of genre, of defining the lines separating, say, "autobiography proper," from the "memoir" or reminiscence (Pascal, 1-20) have, in many instances, been replaced by a greater
recognition of the fluidity between these closely related
autobiographical acts. Pascal's *Design and Truth in Autobiography* is now faulted precisely for its highly rigid and prescriptive definition of autobiography that leads Pascal to
"approve some as "real" and "true" autobiographies while
rejecting others as not "real" or not "true" (Olney, "Autobiography and the Cultural Moment," 12). Olney himself
defines autobiography broadly as "the writing of one's own
life" (*Metaphors of Self*, 35). It is a definition encompassing the

various strains of autobiographical writing, including letters and diaries.

Definitions of "true autobiography" which were grounded in the structure of such works as *Dichtung und Wahrheit* have with few exceptions little relevance for autobiography in the 20th century,[14] leading to the preference of the inclusive term of autobiographical works (Schwab, 16) or autobiographical texts. Such features of self-representation as continuity and harmony in *Dichtung und Wahrheit* stand in contradistinction to the 20th century sense of discontinuity and disharmony. This is particularly true in the case of the exiles whose lives speak of repeated ruptures and discontinuities. In the following chapters the exiles' writings are referred to by the inclusive terms of autobiographical writings and autobiographical texts, or by the exiles' own designation of their work. The influence of earlier models of autobiography are examined in as far as they have been received, adapted or altered by the exiles to suit their own designs as they articulate their particular experiences and philosophical positions.

III

The preoccupation with genre and genre related issues, in creating typologies of autobiographical texts, characteristic of earlier research, has been replaced, in part, by a fascination with such a phenomenon as fiction in autobiography, as well as by a greater interest in new subjects of critical inquiry. The life-stories of individuals and groups, which had previously been condemned to critical amnesia have become one such focal point of recent research. I am speaking of the interest in autobiographies of workers, women, blacks or homosexuals; in brief, texts of the underdog, of the historically disenfranchised, of society's outsiders, texts of the "Other." Clearly, a study treating the autobiographical texts of the exiles can be seen as a reflection of this new interest, for they, too, were the outsiders, the pariahs and disenfranchised whose writings speak of political oppression, tyranny and anti-Semitism. The emerging interest in groups which had not been in the forefront of autobiographical research also coincides with the advent of French Critical Theory.

Katherine Goodman has shown in *Women's Autobiography in Germany between 1790 and 1914* how recent French Critical Theory in its denial of the existence of the author and self poses a threat to the remembering of women's experiences and the constitution of a feminine consciousness. As Goodman points out, while Roland Barthes' writings announced the death of the author, those of Michel Foucault "attempted to bury him" (X). Goodman makes particularly clear that the "very authenticity of the subject women seek in writing — and readers usually seek in their autobiographies — is disputed" (X). Goodman concludes that the "desire to absolutely dismantle the concept of the subject is not in women's interest" (Xii). Her criticism of the deconstructionists could apply equally to Paul De Man and the latter's characterization of referentiality in the autobiographical act as little more than a fiction (De Mann, "Autobiography as De-facement," 920-21). The desire to dismantle the concept of the subject as well as the questioning and rejection of the autobiographer's self-referential gesture is equally not in the interest of the exiles. They, too, were the disenfranchised, the quintessential outsiders. From its beginnings the enterprise of autobiographical research has been concerned with the interpretation and understanding of life. As Wilhelm Dilthey, the father of the study of *Geistesgeschichte* wrote: "Autobiography is the highest and most instructive form in which the understanding of life is revealed to us."[15] The life-stories and experiences of the subjects, the "I's" of the exiles' texts recreate life at the edge, in the abyss, in a new diaspora and have a special relevance for the student of German history, and particularly for the student of exile.[16] To deny the subject in the exiles' texts would be to invalidate their experiences which were linked to some of the most horrific events in the 20th century. Above all, to endorse the assault on and dismantling of the subject and self in the autobiographical texts of the exiles would be to invalidate their experiences and to enter into an alliance with their erstwhile persecutors. For many exiles the autobiographical act was an act of self-assertion, an attempt to give meaning to a life marred by rupture and tragedy. Still, the exiles, particularly the bourgeois intellectuals and writers, were painfully aware that they themselves often bore part of the guilt for the victory of the Nazis and the rupture and discontinuity in their lives. On the other hand, the exiles would inveigh in their texts not only against the agents of Nazism and anti-Semitism, but equally against their sympathizers and supporters, be they in politics, in the judicial system, in industry or art. Confessions of guilt in the face of the Nazi victory in 1933 and accusations against the guilt of others are salient features of the exile's self-representation.

IV

Not since Rousseau has the confessional dimension of autobiography emerged with such force and urgency as in the autobiographical writings of the exiles. Their sense of guilt and their accusations were connected not only with the fate of a single individual, but with the fall of an entire nation into barbarism. Confessions of guilt are to be found in the very first texts to appear after the victory of the National Socialists in 1933. Thus, Ernst Toller attributes in 1933 the Nazi victory to the failed revolutions of 1918 and 1919, but more particularly to the irreconcilable conflicts between Independent Socialists and Communists: "Whoever wishes to understand the collapse of Germany in 1933, has to know the events of the years 1918 and 1919...."[17] The genesis of the Left's defeat during the Revolution of 1918 and 1919 was, in Toller's view, inseparable from their own guilt: "We all failed. We all made mistakes and we are all guilty, the Communists as well as the (Independent) Socialists."[18] For Toller, who was an Independent Socialist and a principal actor in the ill-fated revolutionary government in Munich, the failure of the revolution of 1918 and 1919 was the failure of Communists and Socialists to join forces against the Right, a failure which was, in effect, a harbinger of the victory of National Socialism.

Not only the "politically engaged" remembered and revisited defeat and failure, but more frequently those for whom the prosaic world of politics had been anathema. Their texts are self-incriminatory, texts of self-chastisement: "We, who have betrayed ourselves, carry in the suitcases of our exile Goethe and Hölderlin, Novalis and Kleist. How have we, the heirs, administered this intellectual empire? The notion of freedom, which created all of this, is ruined, the victim of an inane power, and worse than beggars we stand there with our meaningless and useless possessions."[19] Martin Gumpert's *Hölle im Paradies* presents the pitiful images of exiled poets and intellectuals, whose betrayal of the traditions they were called to uphold led to their precarious fate, as beggars on foreign shores.

Looking back in 1941 Klaus Mann questions his contributions as an intellectual to the survival of democracy in Germany—questions which are, in effect, confessions of impotence and failure: "What did I myself do for the improvement and protection of our democracy which so much needed protection and improvement? What was my contribution to the rescue of the imperilled republic? What valiant deed or social accomplishment could I praise myself for?"[20] Likening the Nazis to a modern Hydra, Alfred Döblin confesses: "But what I ask, did I myself really do to destroy it? (One's) aversion (alone) does nothing."[21] Later texts document a continuing preoccupation with the emergence of the Third Reich and the with the question of the bourgeois writer's and intellectual's guilt in the lost struggle against Nazism. Carl Zuckmayer's confession in 1966 is symptomatic of a continuing sense of guilt. It turns on the division and antagonism of art and politics in the Weimar Republic: "We waited too long when our hour and time came to get the upper hand on them....We....waited too long to burden ourselves with the distastefulness of politics. We lived too much in the splendid isolation of the intellect and the arts and thus we, too, share with all Germans a collective shame."[22]

Others, who were deeply involved in the politically tumultuous and chaotic years of the Weimar Republic, treat this "splendid isolation" as an object of derision. The Socialist Toni Sender, observed: "Many so-called intellectuals declared with pride that they were not at all interested in, and were therefore ignorant of politics."[23] To be ensconced in a world of "splendid isolation" did not mean that writers and kindred souls were interested only in aesthetic and theoretical issues. Elisabeth Castonier confesses that she and her circle of friends were blind to the National Socialist threat to the Weimar Republic, a blindness and ignorance inextricably linked to an intensely private existence: "No one in our small circle, who wanted to enjoy themselves dancing and falling in love, had any idea just how far the National Socialist rats had moved forward."[24] Castonier's text mirrors a fixation on private pleasures and an utter disregard for the public sphere, where the bitter struggles between Socialists, Communists and Fascists were waged, whose eventual outcome determined the future fate of the exiles. The exiles' sense of guilt and confessions of guilt go beyond the fall of the Weimar Republic. The flight to safety and the insulation from the horrors that others were destined to experience could likewise become a source of guilt and remorse, even if flight occurred in childhood. Peter Weiss has the protagonist of his autobiographical novel *Fluchtpunkt* confess:

> "For a long time I felt guilty that I didn't belong to those in whose flesh the number of debasement had been burned, that I had escaped and was condemned to be an observer. I had grown up to be murdered, and yet I had escaped destruction."[25]

Not all exile writers and intellectuals felt impelled to confess feelings of guilt in the lost battle against the Nazis. The Communist intellectuals in particular, though some disagreed with Moscow's and the German Communist party's flawed and disastrous tactics for combatting the Nazis, fought to the very end in the struggle against the Nazis and, in many cases, went underground following 1933. On the other hand, bourgeois intellectuals, Communists and Socialists alike would use their texts to accuse others allegedly involved in the debacle of 1933 and its aftermath. To recreate one's life in Germany or Austria in the 1920's and 1930's was to recall the agents of Nazism and anti-Semitism, as well as their sympathizers and collaborators. At the same, the exiles were frequently witness to the betrayal of political ideals and commitments. Such experiences figure prominently in the autobiographical impulse of many exiles, in the imperative to tell and accuse. In recreating her political career in the waning years of the Weimar Republic, Tony Sender accuses Alfred Hugenberg, the chairman of the German Nationalist party and an ally of Hitler for the victory of the Nazis in 1933 and the ensuing reign of Nazi terror and barbarism: "Be it said here: Hugenberg and his party are responsible for Germany's descent into barbarism. They gave the rise of Hitler the outward signs of legality.... Hugenberg introduced the Nazis to the respectable world."[26] While Heinrich Mann accuses the German Industrialists of the Ruhr for financially backing the National Socialists,[27] Klaus Mann accuses Gottfried Benn of a reckless and morally dubious embrace of the "antihumanistic, antichristian radicalism, the irrational vehemence of the Hitler movement."[28]

The exiles' accusations extend beyond the catastrophe of 1933 to the years of flight and the refusal of foreign governments to extend shelter to those fleeing Germany. Egon Schwarz recalls the problematic and frequently fruitless, or even tragic quest of exiles to find a guest country and the indifference and the hostility with which he or she were too often met: "How easy it would have been for the world to have saved all these threatened people. But they refused out of suspicion, hate and selfishness to grant the persecuted shelter...and are partly responsible for the horrible fate that befell so many."[29] The accusations of the exiles are all encompassing and include the moral indictment of countries advocating the policy of appeasement toward Nazi Germany (Cf. Franz Schoenberner, *Bekenntnisse eines europäischen Intellektuellen*, 334). The need to accuse others for the victories of the Nazis not only in Germany, but equally in France finds convincing expression in the autobiographical report *J'accuse*, written by the Communist Otto Katz in 1940 under the pseudonym, André Simone. Katz accuses high officials in the French government of conspiring to break the will of France to fight against Germany. The accusations against French complicity and duplicity, in what would come to be regarded by Left intellectuals and writers as the self-destruction of France, is also articulated in Hans Habe's *Ob Tausend fallen* and Lion Feuchtwanger's *Unholdes Frankreich*.

The sense of betrayal and outrage was even more keenly felt by German Communists who watched with dismay as former comrades deserted the KPD following Hitler's ascension to power.   Writing in his autobiography *Abendlicht* Stephan Hermlin accuses erstwhile Communists of cowardice upon the Nazi takeover (85). On the other hand, the years of exile coincided with the worst of Stalin's purges and the beginnings of a period in which numerous Communists broke with the party, a phenomenon for which the figure of Arthur Koestler became emblematic. The so-called renegades, who figure prominently in the history of exile autobiography, accuse in their writings the Communist party for its betrayal of socialism, or party hacks and careerists for betraying and denouncing their comrades in order to advance their own careers.   Thus Gustav Regler asserts: "Ulbricht betrayed (others) for his own advancement.   Ulbricht denounced rivals in his party.... Ulbricht spied."[30] Political as well as racial persecution figure among the main causes of emigration and exile. The exiles, particularly Jewish exiles, emerge in their texts as the accusers of the prophets and advocates of anti-Semitism, not to mention figures whose rhetoric and actions either directly or indirectly fueled and exacerbated anti-Semitism.   Ludwig Marcuse accuses C. G. Jung for lending intellectual credibility to Nazi propaganda and the persecution of the Jews (Cf. *Mein zwanzigtes Jahrhundert*, 166-173). Fritz Kortner, the celebrated actor and vilified foe of anti-Semitism, accuses the actor Werner Krauss for putting his considerable talents at the disposal of the anti-Semitic campaign of the Nazis (*Aller Tage Abend*, 200).

The exiles' accusations against others, their sense of guilt or confessions of guilt are interwoven into the larger scheme of their self-representation and self-definitions. A closer examination of the exiles' self-representation reveals a larger spectrum, ranging from the presentation of self as religious convert and political crusader, as hero and martyr, to the presentation of the self as the perennial outsider, as victim and as the "Other."   While the exiles' self-representation constitutes one focal point of the following chapters, so too does the exiles' reception of earlier forms and models of autobiography and their departure from conventional autobiographical assumptions and narratives. As noted above, confessions of political impotence and failure permeate the texts of bourgeois intellectuals, while religious confession is a rarity with the exception of Alfred Döblin's *Schicksalsreise, Bericht und Bekenntnis* (1948). In recreating his path to Catholicism, the convert Döblin avails himself of the tradition of confessionary and conversionary autobiography.

PART I

SPIRITUAL AND POLITICAL CONVERSIONS

1

Alfred Döblin's *Schicksalsreise.* *Bericht und Bekenntnis*: Spiritual Crisis and Religious Conversion

Alfred Döblin had experienced the autobiographical impulse long before his exile to France in 1933. But the execution of that impulse, the actual writing of an autobiographical text eluded him for several reasons, ranging, according to Döblin, from the question of age and the autobiographical act to his avowed belief that his life-story contained few exceptional and unique events meriting an extensive autobiographical text (13). Döblin expressed these views in the autobiographical sketch "Ich nähere mich den Vierzig," ("I am approaching forty") which was written around 1920. His early musings on the autobiographical impulse allude to a conception of autobiography whose justification is derived from an exceptional and extraordinary life or a series of events and experiences in one's life—a life replete with "adventurous or original situations...."[1]

In the same text, Döblin recalls his father's desertion of his family, the scourge of poverty, and his continuing sense of being deserted and abandoned to the vagaries of existence. Döblin's longing for a sense of security, for a father who could shield him from the torments and calamities of life also finds expression here. In the following lines Döblin refers not to his mortal father, but to God: "Is there a father to whom one can look up to? It would be comforting if there were. It is bad for someone like me, who is tormented for hours, days, even for months and no one takes him in. A God—it is a wonderful thought."[2] Certainly, from the psychological standpoint Döblin's lifelong search for a superior being in both philosophy and religion was linked to the early loss of his father and his subsequent feelings of deprivation and insecurity (Cf. Prangel, 13). If we are to believe Döblin, God came to him in the form of divine intervention some twenty years later during the German invasion of France and Döblin's flight—his journey of fate, a journey replete with "adventurous and original situations." It was a journey, which, as remembered and reconstructed by Döblin, would justify the writing of an extensive autobiographical text.

Döblin's *Schicksalsreise* is, as its subtitle reads, a report and a confession (*Bericht und Bekenntnis*). It is a report of Döblin's experience of spiritual crisis and religious awakening and a confession of an earlier errant life as well as a confession to God. *Schicksalsreise* is comprised of three books. The first was written in 1941 and titled *Robinson in Frankreich*, alluding to Döblin's sense of initially being stranded on the roads and in the villages of southern France during the German invasion. The title's deeper meaning is linked to Döblin's sense of having reached in France an emotional and spiritual impasse and crisis, which unfolds in his text before the background of the political and military crisis and collapse of France.

In writing the initial book of *Schicksalsreise* Döblin was not only recreating the moments of his crisis and putative religious awakening, but, according to Döblin, returning through the autobiographical act to the wisdom and knowledge that had been revealed to him (116). For the author of *Schicksalsreise* the autobiographical text becomes not only an act of remembering and recreation, but above all, an act of rediscovery—which, once completed, will preserve the pivotal moment in his life: "It is for this reason that I am writing this down. I cannot allow such an extraordinary event to whisk past me like a ray of light."[3] Books II and III were written after his return to Germany in 1945 and relate his confession and formal conversion to Catholicism, and his first experiences in a devastated Germany.

While the literary antecedent of Döblin's conversion and confession to Christianity is to be found in Augustine's *Confessions*, Döblin's text is, in part, reminiscent of Paul's journey to Damascus, his journey of fate, with the exception that it is now not the Jewish persecutor who is converted, but the persecuted Jew and left-wing intellectual Döblin. He had read the great prototype of religious conversion more than once: "After quite some time I once again read the confessions of Saint Augustine...."[4] His reading of Augustine belonged to what Döblin characterized as "a unique learning experience."[5] The reference to Augustine's *Confessions* is made in book II. That Döblin changed the title of the final and enlarged version of his text to *Schicksalsreise* may, in part, be seen within the context of his reading of Augustine's *Confessions*. The image of the journey in quest is central to Augustine's narrative of spiritual crisis and conversion (Fleishman, 62). Augustine's journey, however different from Döblin's in space, time and language, is circular like Döblin's. He moves northward from Thagaste to Carthage, then to Rome, Milan and Cassiciacum and then begins his return home. In the final version of his text, Döblin's journey is understood as beginning with his exile in 1933 which leads him first from Berlin to France, then to America and finally back to Berlin. Similar to Augustine's journey, Döblin's moves in part, within two realms, within an inner and an external world. The journey's of both men as presented in their texts can be seen as the closing of a hermeneutical circle which has led them self-understanding and self-clarity, to a new episteme inextricably linked to Christian eschatology. In fact, Augustine's search for truth, his repudiation of his earlier life as a Manichean, his religious conversion and salvation become a model and touchstone for the seeker Döblin. Moreover, similar to Augustine's, Döblin's inner journey, even after his conversion is an incomplete journey: "This does not end the journey of fate, but what I have to report of it."[6] The final, indeed, penultimate journey for Döblin was, just as for Augustine, the journey to the divine source after death and in perpetuity. In justifying his own conversion, Döblin recreates both his problematical search for truth and security and his failures and debacles in his pre-Christian life. He recalls his reason for studying medicine as being rooted in the desire to know truth (209). As he reinvents it, Döblin's quest for truth, leads him beyond medicine and natural science to philosophy, to Nietzsche, and eventu-

ally to Kierkegaard, each of whom he later rejected: Nietzsche
for his denial of human guilt (225), Kierkegaard because he
was possessed of an unyielding pride (211) blinding him,
Döblin argued, to truth. His early search for truth and what
he regards as the confusions and errors of his life prior to his
religious awakening are set fourth in the chapter "Ich prüfe
und befrage mich" ("I examine and question myself").
Emphasizing at the outset that he wants to come to terms with
his earlier life, Döblin supplies, in effect, the justification or
apology for his religious conversion. As the chapter unfolds, it
moves from self-scrutiny and self-deprecation to self-condem-
nation, often turning on Döblin's alleged inability to truly
commit himself to such religious and political movements as
Zionism and socialism. His travels and writing in behalf of
territorial Zionism, his attempts to learn "Jiddisch" are
recalled, ultimately to be presented as exercises in futility:
"My words did not mean anything here, and I felt nothing.
Again a flag that I could not hold."[7]

The failure to hold the flag of territorial Zionism emerges as
a pattern to be repeated as Döblin recollects his years in Berlin
as a Socialist. He embraced the ideals of socialism, particularly
the basic ideal of a human community promised by socialism
(212). Yet, as he recalls, he was soon repelled by party politics
and party bosses ("Das Bonzentum," ibid). Looking back
Döblin depicts himself as one of the disappointed and disillu-
sioned intellectuals of the Weimar Republic, who, until the
onset of Nazi terror, communed with kindred souls.[8] Disappointment and disillusionment become key features in
Döblin's recreation of a life in which he was unable to make
any cause his own that would give him a sense of identity and
meaning, as well as a sense of security vis à vis the uncertainties and calamities of life. Döblin's accounts of his failed
Zionistic activities and his work for the cause of socialism are
presented in an abbreviated, fragmentary and negative fashion
and are designed to further justify his religious conversion.
He does not include any real details concerning his activities
as a territorial Zionist, nor does he even mention his call for a
spiritual renewal of Judaism. Similarly, he omits a discussion
of his many forcefully and skillfully written political articles

under the pseudonym "linke Poot" which contained his frequently satirical polemic against the reification and bureaucratization of the Left in the Weimar Republic (Cf. Prangel, 37, 82-83).

Döblin was known as one of the most important expressionist writers in Germany. His *Berlin Alexanderplatz* (1929) was destined to take its place among the great novels of 20th century German literature. However, he now portrayed his notable career as a writer largely in a pejorative fashion: "Yes, I also wrote. Did it help me? Did it make me secure? What was it?"[9] Döblin's self-scrutiny speaks of the failure of his writing to bring him what he desired most fervently: help and assurances, indeed, a sense of security in the larger metaphysical context of life. His writing is presented, above all, as an escape, "a silent act behind closed doors,"[10] an escape to exotic lands and different times, in brief, an escape from the realities of his personal life and from the disappointments and his confusion about himself. And yet, his writing, as he recreates it, contained a revelatory and epistemological dimension, for his literary reveries, his wanderings and literary forays into exotic lands often culminated in awakening in him an awe and reverence for what he terms the secret, the *Geheimnis*, underlying the existence of the world (241). The gradual, partial unveiling of that secret occurred, in Döblin"s accounts, in 1940 during his flight through France. As for his alleged failures and disillusionment, his sense of inadequacy, his lack of firm resolution and belief, and his sense of having led a dubious, if not totally false life, these constitute in Döblin's reinvention of his earlier life the main source of his feelings of guilt.

By the time Döblin wrote books II and III of *Schicksalsreise* his religious awakening and conversion lay behind him. He claimed now to have attained a state of self-understanding and clarity about himself. He was able now to decipher a once enigmatic image and vision that allegedly befell him the year before his exile to France. The following passage reveals the interplay of memory and the Christian convert's new perception of that image and vision, both of which are now equated with Döblin's earlier sense of guilt: "I began to see a strange image in 1932....an ancient God, covered with mold, leaves his heavenly abode shortly before his death. A gloomy decree of punishment which he cannot escape forces him onto earth. He is supposed to atone for old sins. And so he wanders through the hot land. What was that? It became clear to me while writing about my babylonian wanderings. It was the feeling of my own lost situation. It was the feeling of guilt...of great guilt. It had become unbearable and did not let up. It was the premonition of exile and much more."[11] Such lines speak unequivocally of Döblin's spiritual crisis, or of a crisis of which he wishes to convince his reader. Its resolution coincides in Döblin's text with the German invasion of France. He remembers his years of exile as years of punishment, in which he atoned for prior sins, for having led an errant existence and for not having sufficiently combatted the rise of Nazism (204). However, he also remembers these years as the years in which his journey to truth and salvation took place, ending his babylonian wanderings and confusion. Exile and particularly its second half, beginning with his flight through France in 1940,[12] are presented in Döblin's text as nothing less than his salvation (368).

He first presents his journey through France in 1940 as a search for his wife and son in the chaotic and perilous days during the German invasion. They had been sent in May from Paris to the south of France, to the town of Le Puy, for their safety. Döblin recalls the he was driven in his search by an impulse – by a feeling of spite, but equally by a seriousness and sadness: "A defeat had come....a great defeat penetrated my being."[13] These lines do not speak of the defeat of France, but present Döblin's sense of personal defeat, his feelings of having squandered so much of his life, and the urge to confront that defeat. The search to locate his family soon becomes in Döblin's recollections a pretense for the personal journey of Döblin in quest for his own fate and salvation (160).

The tension between the protagonist's urge to find his salvation and the desire to locate his family is only resolved after Döblin's religious awakening and a later meeting with his family in Toulouse. The memory of that voyage is, in part, the memory of Döblin's repeated visits to the cathedral in Mende, which have a similar significance as the "garden scene" in Augustine's *Confessions*, where the divine calls and beckons to Augustine. As for Döblin, he recounts his visits to the cathedral as moments when his gaze was directed toward the eternally present crucifix, that is, as moments when a crucified Christ seized his being and would not let go ("Der Gekreuzigte läßt mich nicht los," 224). These visits are characterized by spiritual reveries bordering on hallucinations ("eine...halluzinatorische Erregtheit stellte sich sogar ein", ibid), and by soliloquies in which Döblin comes to accept the meaning of truth of existence as revealed by Christ (245). In brief, they represent the moments of Döblin's epiphany, of his religious awakening and spiritual conversion. At the same time, the presentation of Döblin's religious awakening reflects the interplay and tension of belief and doubt, rapture and skepticism, Döblin's struggle with himself to accept the story of Christ as God and as the son of God, his new belief in God and his fear of an omnipotent God, who allowed the building of concentration camps (188). Döblin suggests that the surmounting of his doubts, was nothing less than an act of God, whose pull on Döblin became irresistible, particularly as Döblin juxtaposed the promise of Christianity with the overwhelming human tragedy and degradation about him, and perceived that man is essentially defenseless against the vicissitudes of life ("widerstandslos gegen alles Mögliche in Gesellschaft und Staat," 223). Clearly, this had been the experience of the exile Döblin, who in seeking refuge and protection from Nazi Germany had, like so many other exiles, fled to France and had become a French citizen, only to experience a few years later the humiliation and defeat of France at the hands of the Nazis.

Döblin's most vivid memory of divine intercession is that of a sudden and unexpected gift of money he received in Marseilles, enabling Döblin and his family to escape from France: "He kept watching me. He did not let go...he interceded."[14] Döblin's story of religious awakening and divine intercession, of his journey to God and truth reaches its climax in the reconstruction of his formal conversion to Catholicism by a Jesuit priest in Los Angeles. The story of Döblin's "journey of fate," is told from the vantage point of a convert who has accepted a Christian view of history and human destiny, and thus a unified conception of the world, history and self: "The world is history, action—and the individual is magnificently involved, there is no death."[15] In the center of that conception is God, the prime mover of history and individual fate. Neither self nor society or an interplay of both were ultimately responsible for human destiny, but rather, according to Döblin, the secret powers which guide man's destiny and which he should not attempt to resist.[16] As Döblin's story unfolds, it becomes sufficiently clear that Döblin is referring in such allusions to no one other than God. From the beginnings of his religious awakening to his memory of God's rescue of himself and his family in France, to his conversion to Catholicism, God is presented as the constant and guiding force in Döblin's life, the only force truly cognizant of the teleology of his existence.

Schicksalsreise culminates in the self-representation of Döblin as a catholic convert and expositor of the faith, as a proselytizer, who attempts to dissuade those committed to a Marxist and revolutionary change of society, arguing that revolutionary politics can only treat the symptoms of man's deeper metaphysical malaise (425).   Of course, many exiles had embraced Marxist revolutionary politics in the Weimar Republic and had joined the German Communist party. A case in point is Gustav Regler whose life-story also speaks of his eventual disillusionment and break with communism.

2

Gustav Regler's *Das Ohr des Malchus*: Political Crusade and Political Conversion in the Autobiography of a Renegade

The student wanting to use autobiographical writings of former Communists as a historical source would need to use Regler's text, like those of most of his fellow renegades, critically and with caution.[1] My purpose here, however, is a different one. I wish to examine Regler's rendering of the course of his life and his understanding of that life as it plays out before the background of social and political upheaval. Regler's *Das Ohr des Malchus* (1958), written at the age of sixty, recreates the stages in the author's life-story. Beginning with his Catholic childhood in the Saar and his service as a soldier in World War I, it progresses to his years in the Communist party, his role in the Spanish Civil War, and finally his break with communism, ending in reflections on his years of exile in Mexico. The autobiography can be read on several levels. Most obviously, it is the story of an individualist in search of social justice, who, like many of his generation, joins the Communist party, to break with it after a period of disillusionment, and to become one of its detractors.

Regler presents his life and career in politics as a series of crusades and defeats, culminating in the defeat of the Republican cause in Spain for which he had fought with the International Brigades and in which he had been severely wounded (205). *The Great Crusade*, the 1940 title given by Regler to his novel on the Spanish Civil War could fit equally Regler's autobiography. He structures his text, in part, as a dialogue, first between himself and his father, later on between himself and his second wife, Marie-Luise Vogeler. Both father and wife serve as alter egos, warning Regler against his involvement in political causes and crusades. The dialogues occur at pivotal moments in Regler's autobiography and deal with the source of a tension running through his entire text. It is a tension only resolved with Regler's later accounts of his political disillusionment and his return to private life during his exile in Mexico (487).

As the story of Regler's often valiant and always perilous career in politics unfolds, so too does his indictment and repudiation of communism and particularly of the Communist party (97). Regler's statement in the appendix to his autobiography that he had tried not to allow "later knowledge" ("verspätete Erkenntnisse," 509), to color chapters dealing with his earlier life in the party and fellow Communists must be read with skepticism. In uncovering his past political career Regler reveals his present vantage point as a detractor of communism, whose criticisms and judgments are the product of a collusion of past and present, the interplay of his memories of earlier experiences with the movement and his present perception of its pitfalls and Machiavellian nature, an understanding, which, however flawed and apologetic it may be, is presented as the result of years of experience and reflection. And thus, Regler, similar to other renegades,[2] emerges in his text as the judge and jury of the Communist party under Stalin, singling out for special ridicule the German Communist party, and such figures and pariahs of contemporary German history as the former East German leader, Walter Ulbricht (Cf. 229-231). Still, Regler's text does not end in a final expression of disillusionment with communism and the self-justification for leaving the party, but rather in a question-mark. Revealing not so much an imperative to condemn or to forgive, he articulates an uncertainty as to who, ultimately has the right to judge: "Who really has the right to judge?"[3]

The question gains its full significance when it is compared with the beginning of his autobiography: a recollection of himself as a young boy of five and of an episode which turns on the fate of a tailor, his impending judgment and fate. The ultimate fate of the tailor remained unknown to Regler, leaving the young and impressionable boy in a troubled state of uncertainty. Thus, Regler's life-story begins with pictures of fear and uncertainty "die Angst....die völlige Unsicherheit" (7-8), and ends with the uncertainties of the sixty-year old. The greater questions involving judgment and fate remain unanswered. Between these two points, the alpha and omega of Regler's text, lies the story of Regler's public and private existence, a story which ends shortly after the recollection of the death of his wife Marie-Luise, culminating in Regler's perceptions of an inexorable chaos permeating life (500). But although Regler's text culminates in a necessarily unanswerable question and in his belief in an unfathomable chaos which rules the lives of men, his self-representation reveals unmistakably the inveterate strategy of an autobiographer who wishes to present himself in the most positive terms.

Regler's life-story was not written by a man inclined to modesty and reticence. Quite to the contrary, his autobiography frequently serves his self-glorification and the justification for his political apostasy. However confused and misguided Regler's life may at times appear to be, depictions of his courage and idealism are central to his self-representation. What his account suggests is a life which exemplifies bravery, a man abhorring cowardice, the story of a personage, who, according to Regler, never feared the power or the wrath of dictators: "I do not fear dictators."[4] This is, according to Regler, what he said in 1934 to Soviet writers upon his first visit to the Soviet Union. Whether accurate or self-serving, his self-characterization evokes the aura of a young hero dedicated to a crusade for social and political justice, no matter what price that crusade would cost in personal terms.

Bravery instead of cowardice, commitment instead of indifference and apathy, protest instead of submission, self-sacrifice instead of self-indulgence emerge as the main qualities of the autobiographical subject. From Regler's rendering of his motives for supporting the Bavarian Revolution in 1919,[5] to his recollections of his defense of Jews in Nürnberg against Streicher's slanderous *Stürmer* (147-48), and Regler's avowed crusade to break down barriers and walls separating and alienating men from each other, (150-51), his image of himself as a political idealist is ever-present. Recalling his best seller *Wasser Brot und blaue Bohnen* (1932), Regler claims that every line in that book was a protest against the inhuman and pernicious prison system of the Weimar Republic (167); and the same idealistic fervor inspired, according to the author, his crusade against the power and decadence of the Catholic Church in his novel *Der verlorene Sohn* (1933).

Regler's decision in 1928 to join the German Communist party is recreated against the background of the late twenties and early thirties, years of mass unemployment, starvation and street warfare in Berlin between Communists, Social Democrats and Nazis. The embracing of revolutionary politics becomes in Regler's self-representation a mark of his compassion and courage. Not to have joined the struggle against hunger and desperation would have been, according to Regler, cowardice (183). Compassion and courage emerge as the key factors in Regler's problematical conversion from the life of the individual to life in the collective, from the religion of Catholicism to the religion of communism. Actually, Regler's ideas for revolution in Germany were, similar to those of his compatriots, shattered by the Nazi victory in 1933 and the totally inadequate Communist response to the victory of Nazism. His memories shift from the lost struggle in Germany to the continuation of the struggle against fascism in exile in Paris, where together with other Communists he contributed to Willi Münzenberg's *Braunbuch*, a scathing indictment of Nazi terror, particularly of the Nazis' burning of the Reichstag (210-11). In recounting such moments Regler invariably interprets them as moments of self-sacrifice, moments when he was willing to sacrifice his private life and personal happiness in the struggle against Nazism. To have given up he finds would have been tantamount to a flight from the collective and its struggle against Hitler and social injustice, an ignominious return to the private sphere.

Regler's odyssey as a Communist exile took him from Paris in 1934 to the Soviet Union, and in the same year to the Saar, which as yet had not been annexed by the Reich. Regler's account of his decision in 1934 to join the struggle against the reunification of Nazi Germany with the Saar once again evokes the image of the undaunted idealist and political crusader. He recalls a conversation with Mikhail Kolzow, an editor at *Pravada*, who, if we are to believe Regler, was amazed that Regler wanted to enter a struggle that had so little prospects of success (234). Once again, this provides the author with an opportunity to present himself not as a Communist tactician and strategist, but as self-sacrificing idealist: "I have never entered a struggle because I was sure of victory."[6] In such recollections principles and idealism are presented as the touchstone of Regler's actions. The memory of his arrival in Saarbrücken, is one of the sight of Nazi uniforms and jackboots, which were so hateful to him that any reservations or fears he might have harbored were, according to Regler, immediately cast aside (300).

Regler's self-representation as a political idealist reaches a high point with the memory of his decision to join the combatants defending Republican Spain in 1936, a unique opportunity to once again prove his bravery and his willingness to sacrifice himself for a greater cause. The guiding principle in his decision was, according to him, that no one has the right to enjoy life while others suffer in misery, to withdraw from the problems of his time, or to desert those who are threatened (359). Yet by the time Regler became a soldier in the International Brigades in Spain he had already entered a period of disillusionment with Soviet communism and its German replica.

Interwoven into Regler's memories of his years as a political idealist and soldier is the story of his disillusionment with communism, and particularly with the excesses of Stalinism. Attempting to understand, and to explain to his reader why he had for so long tolerated the narrowness and shallowness of party politics, Regler conjures up images and memories of his Catholic background, linking lack of protest and abscence of criticism to his Catholic education, with its emphasis on obedience and the need to recognize hierarchies of authority (226). Behind the transparency of Regler's self-scrutiny we discern the words of Regler, the apologist, who attempts to justify his

earlier political illusions and mistakes, particularly his acceptance of Communist dogma. He presents his relationship with
the party as a collision of the individual and idealist with the
cynicism and narrowness of party tactics, where words and
deeds were judged only as means to an end.[7] Although criticism of the party and party politics runs through Regler's text
from the early chapters to Regler's rendering of the party's
harassment of Regler and his wife in Mexico, his actual disillusionment with Stalinist communism is remembered in the context of their journey to the Soviet Union in 1936.

Invited to Moscow by Lev Kamenew, ostensibly to write a
biography of Loyola,[8] Regler and Marie-Luise were witnesses
to one of the darkest hours of Stalinism: The imprisonment of
workers for unpremeditated mistakes on the job (331); the
mistreatment of the displaced Besprisornyje; hunger and pros-
titution, the stifling of private life, the oppression of the
Church and Stalin's ruthless purges of such intellectuals and
fathers of the revolution as Kamenev (354). The journey to
Moscow in 1936 is presented as a pivotal moment in Regler's
political career, a moment shared by his companion and later
wife, Marie-Luise, who Regler recalls as the more perspicacious of the two, particularly in judging communism and the
Soviet Union under Stalin. It is questionable whether Regler
remembered her statements correctly or whether the Marie-
Luise of his autobiography serves as a mouthpiece, voicing and
echoing Regler's own sentiments. Regler's presentation of her
figure could very well reflect the blending of both. At any
rate, Marie-Luise is the second most important figure in
Regler's text, which in its later chapters often oscillates
between his self-representation and a biographical portrait of
Marie-Luise. It is Marie-Luise who sums up the quintessential
lesson of their journey to Soviet Russia in 1936: Socialism
under Stalin was a fraud, "ein Trugschluß" (340). Her incisive
indictments of communism are structured in such a way as to
corroborate and support Regler's premonitions, his growing
doubts and skepticism, his unwillingness to accept the morally
vacuous proposition that the end justifies the means.[9] Moreover, it was Marie-Luise, who in Regler's recollections, made

him realize that all ideologies were responsible for human misery (183).

What may pass as confessions of guilt in *Das Ohr des Malchus*, frequently turns on Regler's relationship to Marie-Luise. He married her in New York in 1940 after having lived with her for thirteen years. She died of cancer during their exile in Mexico. A painter and daughter of the expressionist painter and Communist Heinrich Vogeler, who perished tragically of starvation and exhaustion in 1942 in the Soviet Union, she was, as Regler portrays her, painfully aware of the delusions and pitfalls of political commitment and communism. As noted above, she emerges in Regler's text as his alter ego. He argues that if he had heeded her warnings, the course of their lives would have been much less problematic and tragic. Looking back on what he considers his courageous, but often misguided crusades and struggles, he recalls that his failure to heed her warnings, resulted in calamities and misfortunes which befell both him and and Marie-Luise (162). The inexorable pull of politics and of his political commitments, he claims, entangled Marie-Luise as well in the political vortex and struggles of the Weimar Republic; subsequently in the lost struggle against fascism in exile; and finally in the Communist party's persecution of Regler in Mexico. In her life with Regler, the Communist and later apostate, she would be subjected to physical and psychological rigors, which in Regler's recollections precipitated her disease and ultimately her death.

Regler's memories of Marie-Luise move from her depiction as an astute observer and detractor of political commitment and communism, to the memory of her as the victim of his delusions and crusades. His reflections and ruminations concerning her are frequently accompanied by self-chastisement, remorse and guilt: "Why make the life of a woman so bitter?"[10]....."What right did I have to drag this woman into the hard and problematical life of exile"[11]....."I feel guilty for having enticed her to leave Germany in 1933."[12] Linking the beginnings of Marie-Luise's cancer in Mexico to the Communist denunciation of Regler as a Nazi agent, he writes: "I am certain that her sickness began on this day. She swallowed the poison of disgust."[13]

As he saw it, her death confronted Regler also with a perception of life as chaos; indeed, the chaos precipitated by the infinitesimal cancer cell becomes in a moment of remembered recognition a microcosm of life, a somber metaphor mirroring the quintessence of existence, the chaos ubiquitously present beneath life's surface, beneath an illusory order of things. Regler's memory of Marie-Luise's painting in Mexico is the memory of an artist's fleeting victory over the dark side of life, "of color over darkness, of gentleness over brutality, of harmony over the chaos of the cancer cells."[14] Still, in the end the deadly chaos of the cells vanquish Marie-Luise, the chaos which in Regler's text permeates life, and whose ominous manifestations we repeatedly encounter in Regler's autobiography (Cf. 82, 154, 469). The intertwining of this recognition and Regler's perception and observation of the timeless simultaneity of life's joys and its miseries, of man's wealth and poverty, of bliss and suffering emerge as fragments and indices of the greater truth governing life. In light of these experiences who did, in fact, as Regler asks toward the end of the text, have the right to judge?

However, in addition to the memory of Marie-Luise's tragic death to cancer and the party's harassment of the apostate, Regler's autobiography also recounts his and Marie-Luise's turn to mysticism and immersion in Indian culture and their need to cast away the memories of the past "like filthy bandages."[15] This foray into mysticism is recreated by Regler as yet another turning point in his peripatetic life (485). Perceptions of timelessness, limitlessness and reincarnation are interwoven in his memories and musings on the new course his life was then taking with Marie-Luise before her fatal illness. Written at the height of the Cold War, the autobiography evokes in its final pages the specter of renewed warfare. Recalling his return to a Europe in 1957 still bearing the visible scars of war and overshadowed by the threat of a more deadly conflict, Regler asks, if history is about to repeat itself: "Is it really about to begin again?"[16]

The tone of the question is one of resignation and pessimism, a question uttered by a man whose life-story reads as a valiant but failed crusade to change the world. Was he, Regler asks at one point, in fact, a victim of his own desires ("War ich wirklich ein Opfer meiner Wünsche?", 294). Read within the context of this question Regler's account is the story of a man's quest and crusade to change the world and his collision with the timeless and inexorable realities of the world. Such a reading would fit in with Regler's strategy of presenting his life as one of courage and heroism, his self-justification and his moments of self-glorification.

However, in reconstructing his past life, Regler also sought to gain clarity about his life in the greater scheme of things. His reflections and musings at the end of his autobiography reflect his perceptions of life as a dialectic of happiness and misery. Man's misery is, in Regler's reflections tied, of course, to many things, and ultimately to the chaos which manifests itself in the biological and political life of the human species. In a rare moment of reflection on the vicissitudes of history that takes place in the context of Regler's recreation of his internment in Le Vernet after the Spanish Civil War, he characterizes history as the "manifestation of human inadequacy."[17]

Excursus:
History and Exile Autobiography

It is no coincidence that the exiles whose lives were threatened and ravaged by the course of 20th century history repeatedly return in their texts to reflections on and interpretations of history. In the following I will refer to only a few of these texts. Many others could also be cited. Elisabeth Castonier recalls the insecurities and anxiety the exile felt as he or she awaited the next turning point of history ("wohin die Weltgeschichte uns treiben würde" *Stürmisch bis heiter. Memoiren einer Außenseiterin*, 279). Although Willy Haas assures his reader that his intention is not to write an historical book, he must also confess that reflections on history cannot be excluded from his text (*Die literarische Welt. Erinnerungen*, 17). The attempt to focus on one's private and personal life as opposed to analyses of 20th century history is reflected in the title of Ludwig Marcuse's autobiography *Mein zwanzigtes Jahrhundert*. Marcuse even proclaims that world history itself does not exist (376); but his own disillusionment, of which he readily speaks, stems from his experience of and reflections on history.

Turning points and cleavages in history in the ruminations of the exiles can include every significant chapter in 20th century history, from World War I to the Cold War. Some of these reflections present the individual as a hapless object and victim of history, for whom the notion of the freedom of the individual to determine his or her destiny appears at best to be an illusion. Egon Schwarz, who is preoccupied in his autobiography with the problem of individual freedom, describes his life, his *bios*, as a kind of plaything of historical forces ("eine Art Spielball geschichtlicher Mächte" *Keine Zeit für Eichendorff. Chronik unfreiwilliger Wanderjahre*, 2). Clearly, one of the most alarming portents of history was the emergence of unbridled anti-Semitism.   Recreating his dismissal from a Gymnasium in Vienna at the hands of an anti-Semitic student body, Schwarz writes not without irony: "World history deprived me of a more intimate acquaintance with this venerable institute".[1]

Schwarz recreates the ruptures in his early childhood and education and their precipitation by history's descent into barbarism. Other exiles reflect on history's devastating effects on their career and personal fortunes. An instance is the autobiography of the former Communist, Julius Hay, whose career as a promising young playwright in Berlin ended like that of many other young artists with the Nazi victory in 1933, and Hay's subsequent flight and exile.   Having recounted his initial success in 1932 as a dramatist, Hay concludes: "I would (like) to tell this story as it could have continued, yes, as it would have had to continue, if my evil companion, the 20th century, had not muddled everything."[2] In Hay's autobiography 20th century history emerges with all the trappings of a demonic adversary, who abuses and torments his victim. Almost every disappointment and tragic turn in Hay's life is ascribed to its course. The specter and legacy of history takes on the contours of rhetorical construct. He refers to it either as "my evil or malicious companion" (Cf. 119, 133).   Hay's rhetorical use of "demon history" serves to rationalize his own misjudgments and sense of guilt, both in his personal and political life.

The autobiographical reflections of the exiles centering on the dialectics of history move from the recounting of one's victimization at the hands of history, to interpretations of the great catastrophes and lost opportunities for lasting peace and stability in a century which was sliding ever-more quickly into the fascist abyss.   For Stefan Zweig 20th century history becomes the memory of a "catastrophic sequence of events whose witnesses and victims our generation has been since 1914...."[3]   In his "World of Yesterday" Zweig looks back not only nostalgically to a lost golden age of European peace and security, but also interprets 20th century history's descent into fascism. Zweig emphasized that his work would not contain "much of private things" but rather... "a large outlook"

(Quoted in Prater, *European of Yesterday*, 301). And indeed, Zweig's presentation minimizes the private aspects of his life in favor of a broadly conceived retrospective predicated on the perception of the 20th century's relentless destruction of civilization. Zweig's strategy, linked to the exile's preoccupation with the course of history, is shared by Heinrich Mann, whose optimistic, if not utopian interpretations of history posit, however, the antithesis to Zweig's pessimism.

In Mann's autobiographical work *Ein Zeitalter wird besichtigt* (1946) a space once filled by self-representation is occupied largely by forays into history, by the unearthing of the genesis and artifacts of fascism and German aggression. The dynamic of Mann's text marginalizes the story of self and individuality. Ultimately, Mann's work is not so concerned with the writing of "my history" than it is with that of Germany's and Europe's-still unfolding history-since the French Revolution. At the same time, he is also concerned with the great men of the 19th and 20th century—the movers and architects of history. For exiles subscribing to a purely Marxist interpretation of history it was clear that history was moving ineluctably toward a global socialist order (Cf. Leonhard Frank's *Links wo das Herz ist*, 258-259). Future and anticipation also play a prominent role in Klaus Mann's *Der Wendepunkt*. The title of Mann's text alludes to the turning points in his life-story. However, the last turning point discussed in the enlarged German version deals with the postwar era and the political polarization of East and West. What Klaus Mann perceived in the postwar era was not the inevitability of historical progress, but the possible destruction of the individual and collective history, the end of bios. In the final pages of his autobiography Mann calls the end of World War II "a great day, a turning point in history."[4] Yet, his pleasure at witnessing the collapse of the Third Reich is tempered and overshadowed by anxiety, by the specter of a war that could, in fact, end all wars: "Now (history) will continue, the question is in which direction it will continue....We can decide for the right direction or for the false (direction). The wrong direction will become increasingly wrong, increasingly dangerous. A few more steps toward the precipice and we will fall in. The final turning point would be reached. The episodic drama will have ended."[5] As Klaus Mann saw it, the only hope for mankind was a genuine understanding between the East and the West: "Each step which leads us away from this goal, leads us to the abyss."[6] In the final pages of his autobiography Klaus Mann is less concerned with articulating a final judgment on the life he has led — notably, his own development from an aesthete to a militant humanist and a soldier in the United States Army, as he is with the historical process, and the new crises and turning points in history.

As the exile autobiographer moves into the postwar period, his or her life now unfolds before the specter of a nuclear cataclysm. In the age of anxiety the texts of the exiles reflect a change in perspective; no longer only confessionary and accusatory, they issue timely warnings against the new and ominous contours of history-history's possible descent into a new abyss. The exile autobiographer, who was once preoccupied with the collapse of the Weimar Republic and the victory of the Nazis in 1933, now takes on the role of a latter day Cassandra. Sharing Klaus Mann's somber prognosis for the future Fritz Kortner looks with trepidation into the next chapter of his life as a future threatened by the apocalypse (57). The justification of one's existence is now seen by such figures as the left-wing journalist Bruno Frei in the intellectual's struggle to move history away from nuclear war: "The literary and journalistic campaign for men's minds will determine whether nuclear war will occur throughout the continents."[7]

PART II

THE MARGINALIZATION AND EXALTATION OF SELF AND INDIVIDUALITY

3

Heinrich Mann's
Ein Zeitalter wird besichtigt:
Inscribing Historiography and
Biography in the Autobiographical
Act or the Marginality of
Self and Individuality

Heinrich Mann's autobiography was completed well before the
dropping of the first atom bomb, a few days after D-Day in
1944, at a time when the alliance between the Soviet Union
and the West seemed to promise not only the destruction of
Nazism, but a continued understanding between the rival
camps of Communism and the Western Capitalist democra-
cies — the advent of a new world order anchored in the continuing alliance between the West and the Soviet Union. At seventy-three, the author saw the waning of his own life-story as
coinciding with the end of an age marked by irrationalism and
German aggression.

His text, concerned, above all, with the interpretation of the
historical forces which shaped his own century, constitutes the
antithesis of the self-glorification and exhibitionism that had
become one of the marks of autobiography since Rousseau, as
illustrated above in the account of Gustav Regler. As implicit
in the very title of Mann's work, and documented by a letter to
Alfred Kantorowicz in 1943, he was less interested in his own
self-representation than in reviewing the age.[1] The writing of
his life-story, he claimed, was merely a pretense for writing
contemporary history ("mit meiner Existenz als zufälligen

Anlaß", *Ein Zeitalter wird besichtigt*, 572). Several important moments in his biography, including his childhood were simply omitted from his text.

The desire to view and understand one's age in the autobiographical act was first articulated and practiced by Goethe in *Dichtung und Wahrheit*.[2] For Goethe an understanding of oneself was inseparable from understanding the age in which the self had developed and continued to develop in a process ending only with death. The intersection of the self and historical circumstance, and the molding of the self in its interplay with the historical forces of its age are characteristic of Goethe's text. This is equally true of Mann's work. Mann's particular outlook at the age of seventy-three reveals an often contradictory blending of resignation, pessimism and optimism, all bearing the indelible imprints and effects of the historical catastrophes of an age of irrationalism, as well as history's promise of a new world order of universal peace and security.

Still, the interplay of self and world, as exemplified by the Goethean paradigm, has given way in Mann's *Ein Zeitalter wird besichtigt* to a marginalizing of the self and its story and a corresponding preoccupation with historical reflections, including biographical portraits of the major historical personalities of the time, from Bismarck to Churchill. As for the self, it is only introduced into the text after some hundred and fifty pages: "It's time that I introduced myself. My name is Jx."[3] Mann's choice of the name, or more precisely the letters Jx, speak of a desire of anonymity, a desire normally alien to a the writers of autobiography who wish to present the uniqueness and singularity of their life-stories. In fact, Mann's further introduction of Jx amounts to a tour de force of self-effacement. It is not uniqueness and singularity he points to when describing himself but rather, similarity, likeness, even sameness: "My kind appears everywhere...everyone should be able to think and do what I can."[4]

Writing with regard to the imminent allied victory, Mann states: "Jx, the countless persons with this name are supporting the victors of this war."[5] In short, Jx stands for the countless supporters of the Allies, to whom Jx belongs and of whose fate, suffering and hopes he is representative. To be sure, the same countless Jxs have suffered from and been subjected to the barbarity of the Third Reich (153). The image of countless Jxs is continually evoked in passages of the text dealing with Mann's personal biography: "Jx thinks—many Jxs think."[6] Thinking of the Soviet Union and its promise to combat fascism and ultimately to destroy the seeds of fascism and war is a thought and hope that Mann shared with countless Left intellectuals. Reflecting on his own ruminations on the dialectics of history, its retrograde moments as well as its progress towards a new age of reason, Mann asserts that these reflections constitute, in fact, a continuum, in which other and more important voices than his have expressed themselves: "The same conversations took place between other Jxs, who are dead, but are more important."[7]

Mann's self-representation as Jx seems nonetheless curious, and even enigmatic. Clearly, Heinrich Mann's life, his career and accomplishments were unique and exceptional beyond any doubt. The author of famous novels of social criticism, ranging from *Professor Unrat* (1905) to *Der Untertan* (1918), served during the Weimar Republic as the chairman of the Section for Literature in the Prussian Academy for Arts, virtually as the official literary representative of the republic. He assumed a position of intellectual leadership and moral authority among German speaking exiles in France,[8] and served there as chairman of the German Popular Front. Writing for the "Depêche de Toulouse" between 1933-1940 he attempted to become the conscience of a progressive France in the face of Nazi pressure and power, admonishing the French to reject the seduction of fascism. However, in speaking of these activities, Mann always does so from the vantage point of a defeated writer forced to embark on the journey into exile (Cf. 376, 387).

Mann's initial assertion that his kind appears everywhere and that anyone should be able to do what he does speaks unequivocally of his democratic and egalitarian leanings, his rejection and repudiation of the bourgeois idealization of the individual and its self-assertion and self-representation in the genre of autobiography. His self-characterization as Jx can be read as a rejection of the late 18th and 19th century autobio-graphical ideal of "individuality," and indeed the traditional conception of autobiography as trajectory of the *bios* of an individual, from which it has derived its justification for much of its history as a literary genre.   Mann claims: "An Auto-biography does best by ignoring its author....He should appear as a witness to events....and of himself."[9]   Mann's conception of autobiography implies a shift of perspective and focus from an exclusive rendering of the story of the self to the historical events and world about the self.

Although Jx may introduce and speak of himself, he should only do so in a limited fashion ("mit Maßen," 149).   Mann's reluctance to focus on the details of his life-story is also linked to his belief that the age must be closely examined and inter-preted, because it has formed in large measure the outlook of the autobiographer: "The age in which he is involved inter-prets him...."[10]   In brief, the historical and political realities of the age tell us why Mann believes and feels the way he does. Mann continues by asserting that the idea of himself is, in fact, his invention (Ibid).   The idea of himself alludes, of course, to Mann's belief in his calling as a writer and an intellectual, one whose mission has been to politically and morally enlighten his contemporaries; to reveal and denigrate Germany's de-scent into social and political barbarism.   In the unfolding pages of his text the idea of the self is translated largely into the story of the self, the story of the morally and politically engaged writer.

As recreated by Mann, his story as a writer combatting the reactionary forces in the Wilhelmian Reich, and engaged in literary campaigns against fascism, is one of failure and resig-nation.   Recalling his earlier novels of social criticism and protest, he writes; "Was I a fighter? I described what I saw and I attempted to...demonstrate my knowledge and to make it useful."[11]   As for his journalistic writing for the *Depêche de Toulouse* he states: "...I reached everything that I wanted to with people who were of my opinion, (but) seldom did we con-vince others."   At an earlier point in the text and speaking of Jx, Mann emphasizes: "I find it inexcusable that he couldn't change anything."[12]   Recalling his departure from exile in

France, Mann speaks of how the politically and morally engaged writer who has failed in his mission seeks refuge in anonymity: "Whoever departs and does not leave anything behind except disaster, seeks comfort, even justification in anonymity...."[13]

It could be said that the story of Mann's development as a writer and an intellectual culminates not only in the reflections on the need to falsify one's identity, but in a gradual yet inexorable loss of identity, which had first been threatened with his exile to France and was vastly diminished at the moment of his departure from Europe. As Mann's text remembers the self, it moves from the story of Jx's failed career as a political writer to the memory of Jx's quest for anonymity, a quest to literally save the life of the exile Jx, but equally a quest, whose fulfillment, if we are to believe Mann, constituted the promise and comfort of a new, albeit, false identity. Mann's presentation of what he terms his failed career as a politically engaged writer bears the unmistakable mark of self-doubt. These doubts and Mann's skepticism with regard to his accomplishments, his rejection of his specific individuality and the narrowing and closing of his world make his text almost the antithesis of the paradigm of autobiography canonized by Goethe's *Dicthung und Wahrheit*.[14]

Mann's departure from France amounted, in effect, to a continuation of the ruptures and discontinuities in his life, precipitated initially by his exile from Germany in 1933. His text fuses the past, the present and the future in the story of an age which began with peace and which will, with the defeat of Nazism, culminate in a new era of peace. The images of his youth in Bismarckian Germany reflect not merely nostalgia, but rather present an ideal period of individual development, a time whose stability was inextricably linked to the policies of Bismarck: "He not only maintained peace from 1875-1890, but he ... strengthened peace. Thank's to the Prince peace was able to continue another twenty-five years in spite of arrogance and ill will."[15] Reflecting upon his youth, Mann perceives in this enduring peace the basis for the continuity of individual development: "In order for a young person to develop in a coherent fashion, to develop, to use an expression of the 19th century, historically, he has to believe that the course of his life is anchored in a logical scheme of things, which ceases if there is war. Wars are the violent rupture in a life which had otherwise been connected."[16] Luxuriating in the memory of his youth, Mann extols the virtues of Bismarck, who emerges in Mann's renderings as a moralist and an intellectual par excellence (476). Mann's portrait of Bismarck marks the beginning of his idealization of historical personalities by way of a mixture of fact and fiction. These include Churchill, Roosevelt and Stalin, whose political policies and social programs held the promise in Mann's view of returning peace and security to the world. It is almost as if Mann sees his age as a historical triad, beginning with the period of Bismarckian peace, followed by the beginnings of an age of irrationalism under Wilhelm the II, reaching its zenith under Hitler, which is then eclipsed by the advent of a new age, championed by Churchill, Roosevelt and Stalin—an era of peace under the aegis of communism.[17]

In Mann's presentation of the great political personalities of the 20th century autobiography gives way to biography. Self-invention and self-justification are supplanted by the idealization and fictionalization of the Allied Leaders, and by the justification and defense of their actions and policies. Mann's ideal of moral and intellectual leadership becomes the mark of Churchill, Roosevelt and Stalin. At the same time, his analysis of the Allied Leaders reflects not only the interplay of fact and fiction, but his attempt to wed biography with autobiography. Having termed the Allied Leaders intellectuals and moralists, statesmen who are committed not only to defeating Hitler, but to ending poverty and want in their respective countries, he concludes by identifying their programs and ideals with his own.[18] In doing so, Mann asks the rhetorical question: "These are impersonal questions? They are the most personal."[19] In the end, the images Mann presents of the Allied Leaders mirror his own personal and moral commitments, and thus his own *bios*. For as he puts it: "My...life completely depends on whether moral endeavors are possible."[20]

Originally, in 1941 Mann entitled his work "Zur Zeit von Winston Churchill" (At the time of Winston Churchill). The

English Prime Minister emerges in *Ein Zeitalter wird besichtigt* as an heroic figure, "ein Held von Corneille" (87), whom fate itself has called forth in the defense of England, and what is more, as a statesman who intends to follow the moral example of the Soviet Union in the quest to end poverty and human degradation (74). According to Mann, the Soviet Union represents for Churchill the acknowledged state of the age, the only one which moves beyond the age and at the same time leads the age. Moreover, Mann's ideal statesman, who is steeped in literature, finds its expression in his presentation of the British leader: "The statesman Churchill has his roots in the writer, Churchill."[21]   Knowledge of literature was, according to Mann, the *sine qua non* for effective political leadership (315). As for Roosevelt, he is, Mann contends, the most intellectual leader the Americans have ever known (32). In supporting his views that Churchill and Roosevelt have begun to emulate the Soviet Union, he points to Churchill as the advocate of a new and equitable system of social security (459-463), and to Roosevelt's commitment to fight and eradicate poverty (493).

In his biographical reflections on Churchill the latter's earlier and extreme anti-Soviet stance before the war remains unacknowledged in Mann's text. Mann depicts the English leader not necessarily as he was, but as Churchill and England should be: a statesman and a country which have embarked on the long march to communism. In drawing parallels between Churchill and Roosevelt and earlier leaders Mann turns to his historical novel *Die Vollendung des Königs Henri Quatre* (1935): "I knew King, Henri Quatre of France. He wanted the same things (for his subjects)...as Mr. Churchill and Roosevelt."[22] In Mann's portrayal Henri Quatre's quest as a sovereign is seen as a quest devoted to both the bringing about of religious freedom and the creation of a nation without poverty (*Henri Quatre II*, 981). The linking of Churchill and Roosevelt with Henri Quatre reflects the blending of fact and fiction, the fashioning of historical figures to correspond to Mann's image of ideal statesmen, intellectuals and moralists whose very justification as leaders is seen not only in defeating Hitler, but in ending poverty.

Mann is equally, or even more effusive in his praise of Stalin, assuming at times the role of an apologist for the Soviet leader. Self-justification in the autobiographical act now gives way to the biographer's justification of the morally dubious and questionable acts of his subject, particularly Stalin's infamous purges. These are interpreted by Mann as an act of self-defense and the moral armament of the Soviet people against the forces of counter-revolution (111). As for the 1939 pact of non-aggression between the Soviet Union and Nazi Germany, Mann concedes that he was initially shaken by its possibly ominous meaning. In describing his first reactions to the pact, he stresses its universal nature: "I experience nothing other than (what) the people do. They undoubtedly felt like I did.... The report of the pact—of treason, of catastrophe—shocked me like everyone."[23] Still, he procedes to present the pact as solely a defensive maneuver, giving the Soviet Union much needed time to prepare for the inevitable Nazi attack (127).

In addition to biographical portraits and autobiographical reflections, Mann's text contains most importantly his reflections on the dialectics of history. The autobiographer as historiographer commands from the very outset a preeminent position in Mann's text. The unmasking and decoding of the riddles of the age, the penetration of the age's historical genesis, particularly the origins of the catastrophe of World War II, permeate his work: "There are connections, one can decode them provided that one had been present at that time, and had lived long enough afterwards."[24] Still, Mann's interpretation of the etiology of German fascism and aggression goes beyond the beginnings of his own age: "I...know that the connections extend far into the past."[25]

Mann claims that the roots of 20th century German aggression, are to be found in the collision of Germany and France at the beginning of the 19th century, which he interprets as a collision of the progressive and emancipatory forces of history with its reactionary and retrograde forces. The genesis of Germany's current aggression is traced to Germany's need for revenge for past defeats and humiliations, beginning with the Napoleonic conquests and extending to Germany's defeat in World War I. In Mann's reinvention of German history revenge is coupled with imitation, the imitation of Napoleon and Napoleonic victories, whose inception Mann situates at the moment of Germany's own wars of liberation against Napoleon (16). Revenge and imitation are presented by Mann as the constants of German history and as forces which have precipitated the ruptures and discontinuities in Mann's life as well as a threat to his life.

As Mann, the historiographer, unmasks and reinvents German history, the Wars of Liberation against Napoleon emerge as wars of revenge, but also of containment and destruction of the emancipatory forces of the French Revolution in Germany (20). Given Mann's allegiance to the Soviet Union and the widespread belief among Left intellectuals in the Twenties and Thirties that the Soviet Union was the rightful heir to the emancipatory forces of the French Revolution,[26] it was only logical that Mann would present the Soviet Union in that very light (119). As stated before, the Soviet Union is regarded by Mann as the exemplary state, whose social policies are being emulated by Britain and the United States. The Soviet Union's commitment to communism is, in Mann's portrayal, a commitment to morality; and thus to the same cause that Mann describes as central to his career as a writer. Mann's invention of past and current history in a manner to make it correspond to his deeply and long held beliefs and commitments leads finally to his anticipation of a future age of social justice, ending poverty and thus signaling an end to wars, and therewith an end to the discontinuities and ruptures in the lives of men and women. Mann's text culminates in his invention of a metamorphosis of the Western Allies, guided and prodded by the example of the Soviet Union: "A new man, a new age begins here."[27]

Even so, the ending of Mann's text reflects a mixture of hope in the future course of history and of resignation with his own failure to affect political and social change: "I view an age....It has amounted to more than I have."[28] On the other hand, immediate postwar history, particularly the polarization of the West and East and the ensuing Cold War, can be read as a refutation of Mann's perceptions and invention of the future course of history. However cogent and perspicacious many of

Mann's analyses may be of his age, he must confess to the limitations of individual knowledge. The memory of the exile's departure from France is not only bitter because of the catastrophe he is leaving behind, but because he is never able to discover the whole truth ("die ganze Wahrheit," 449), the truth about the catastrophes of his own age and the truth behind his own failings in the lost struggle against fascism in Europe. In the end, it is the ever illusive truth regarding the interplay of an intellectual and his age, their reciprocal influence in the unfolding dialectic of history.

Although, Mann text's is characterized by frequent self-deprecations and self-effacement — by his alleged failings as a writer, his own salvation as well as that of his contemporaries is perceived in the ineluctable march of history, in the realization of a new age of reason and a new world order of peace and security in a world without poverty. These utopian visions are similar to the visions in which the historical novel *Henri Quatre* culminates. Most importantly, their translation into word and text reflects the creation of fictions. Indeed, self-invention gives way in Mann's *Ein Zeitalter wird besichtigt* to the fictionalization of historical personalities, to utopian perceptions and inventions of history.

4

Ludwig Marcuse's
Mein Zwanzigstes Jahrhundert:
Combatting the Tyranny of
Historiography or the Exaltation of
Self and Individuality

A first reading of Ludwig Marcuse's *Mein zwanzigstes Jahrhundert* (1960) could easily leave the impression that it is,in large part, a text dealing with 20th century literary history, presented within the framework of the memoir. In light of the numerous references to literary movements like Expressionism and New Objectivity, and the biographical and interpretive sketches of literary figures,this view does not altogether seem to be without merit.[1] Still, Marcuse himself asserts: "I am not writing here literary history, not even a history of the exiled literati."[2] To be sure, Marcuse's text contains far more than the memories of fellow exiled writers, however intrinsically valuable such memories may be. *Mein zwanzigstes Jahrhundert* is written from the perspective of a militant individualist and an incisive critic of the intrusion of politics into the private sphere of the individual, a development which Marcuse traces back to the middle of the 19th century and one he sees as reaching far into the second half of the 20th century. *Mein zwanzigstes Jahrhundert* thus constitutes the antithesis, if not the disparagement of the life-story as political crusade, and even more so of historiography's fixation on the great actors and men of history.

Marcuse's text moves from the titillating memories of private pleasures to a defense of the sanctity of the individual in

an age which, according to Marcuse, is hostile to the philosophy of individualism. Marcuse's provocative attack on the
intrusion of politics into the private sphere is aimed, above all,
at the herald of revolution and the collective and for Marcuse,
the gravedigger of the private life of the individual, namely
Karl Marx. These polemics against Marx culminate in *Nachruf
auf Ludwig Marcuse* (1969), Marcuse's necrology on himself, the
sequel to his autobiography, and the final condemnation of
the man who was, in Marcuse's view, more effective than any
idealist before him in creating contempt for the private life of
the individual (*Nachruf*, 39). In defining his own philosophical
roots in romanticism and in the philosophy of individualism
Marcuse alternatively satirizes and pillories Marx and the
threadbare cliches of vulgar Marxism: "At least in my life consciousness did not follow existence."[3] Along with Marx, Marcuse's polemics against the foes of the individual and individual freedom encompasses Hegel and generally the emergence
of historical determinism with its assault on the ideal of a free
and self-determining individual and therewith the centrality
of the individual (376-377).

Marcuse emphasizes the importance of the life-stories of
forgotten individuals, who, because of their supposed insigni-
ficance for the march of history, are condemned to historical
oblivion, to the unwritten pages of history. It is such a story,
Marcuse asserts, that he is writing in *Mein zwanzigstes Jahrhundert*: "I am telling one of those life-stories which, according
to Hegel, are to be found on the empty pages of the great book
of memory (world history). In contrast to Hegel, these
millions of empty pages seem more notable to me than the
printed ones."[4] In remembering and recreating the course of
his *bios*, Marcuse is, in effect, rescuing the self, whose singular
and unique story, if untold, is destined to be overshadowed
and forgotten. Remembering the self in the autobiographical
act, but equally rescuing the self from the threat of oblivion
merge in a text which never ceases to proclaim the singularity
of the individual, Ludwig Marcuse.

In protesting the stigmatization of the individual and of singularity in a politicized and materialist age, Marcuse finds that
singularity and individuality are either eschewed or viewed

with discomfort, if not disdain. He speaks of "the uneasiness of the individual with his singularity."[5] In keeping with his bias, he rejects autobiographies of the great men of history, which are further flawed, in his view, by their tendency to neglect the private and individual world of the autobiographer: "The great man does not write an autobiography, but world-history in so far as he is identical with it."[6] Accoridng to Marcuse, the writing of individual history must begin by focusing exclusively on the individual's life. True autobiography can never center on external accomp-lishments, but only on the self "nur das Selbst" (*Nachruf*, 35).

Marcuse's fixation on the self and the private, and his recurring pronouncements that the private is the domain of autobiography, is designed to challenge reader expectations in a politicized era in which autobiography and the memoir have increasingly merged, and autobiography is often read as a reflection of political and cultural history. Moreover, he readily identifies himself with the romantic philosophers, with Stirner, Schopenhauer, Kierkegaard and Nietzsche: "I have always believed...that despite all world-history, the world begins and ends with the individual."[7] That belief was influenced particularly by Marcuse's study of Nietzsche and his later readings of the solipsist and renegade Young Hegelian, Max Stirner. As for Marcuse's affinity for Nietzsche, it would lead to the writing of his dissertation in 1917 with the revealing and instructive title *Die Individualität als Wert und die Philosophie Friedrich Nietzsches*, a study which portrays Nietzsche as a militant individualist (48). According to Marcuse, it was from Nietzsche that he would learn that the individual and not God or nature, or the category of reason is at the heart of the world (49). As for Stirner, who also plays a key role in the unfolding story of Marcuse's education, his famous and infamous dictum: "I am solely interested in myself."[8] could serve as an appropriate subtitle for Marcuse's autobiography. Returning in *Nachruf auf Ludwig Marcuse* to the often maligned prophet of individualism, Marcuse observes that Stirner's writings are true in their fervent protest in favor of the unique individual and in their emphasis on the centrality and importance of the individual's private existence (38).

The title of Marcuse's autobiography speaks unequivocally of his intention to tell the story of his personal century, particularly of his private, albeit erotic life, as it unfolds before the great political upheavals and catastrophes of the age. He presents himself particularly in his earlier years prior to exile as an at times successful and at times failed, worshipper and devotee of pleasure, ensconced in a world of erotic pursuits. The juxtaposition of public and private interests, of political events and eroticism, and the enthroning of the private over the public is a hallmark of Marcuse's text.

Revolutions like wars are, Marcuse asserts, private affairs. While the November Revolution of 1918 in Germany may have shaken many, it did nothing to him. On the ninth of November 1918, when the German revolution began, Marcuse recalls he spent a most fulfilling ("abenderfüllend") time with an actress (*Mein zwanzigstes Jahrhundert*, 47). As for 1919, the year of the founding of the Weimar Republic, all Marcuse can or wants to remember is that he said goodby to one of his lovers, thereby avoiding a marriage and was able to deepen yet another relationship: "I loved G. B. more than ever before ....On the other hand, Scheidemann und Ebert lived only on the periphery of my world. I cannot tell the reader anything about them, although I am sure that it would interest him (but why should it?)"[9] The parenthetical question is at once a challenge to and a criticism of reader expectations.

Of course, the year 1919 was politically a watershed year, as Marcuse recalls, including the founding of the Weimar Republic and the Communist International, Arthur Dintner's anti-Semitic novel, *Die Sünde wider das Blut*, Chamberlain's *Rasse und Nation* and the founding of the German Workers Party, the nucleus of the later Nazi party. However, such events serve merely as a colorful foil, however ominous. In comparing them with his private life, Marcuse proclaims: "But all of this did not belong to my year of 1919."[10]

Clearly, Marcuse must concede that some of the political events in the year 1919 such as the general strike of the Communist Spartacus Alliance did touch him. The memory of this event is conjured up not so much for its political significance, but because it caused Marcuse to move to a suburb of Berlin, where there resided, he recalls, a second cousin, in whose presence he was able to forget the unfolding events of history ("die mir die gleichzeitige Weltgeschichte stark in den Hintergrund drängte", 56). As for the portentous years of 1923 and 1924, they found Marcuse in Munich and Barcelona, but his thoughts, so he tells his reader, were not on Hitler and Ludendorff nor on Primo de Rivera, but rather on the woman whom he refers to as *a*: "She ruled my years 1923 and 1924.... Hitler and Ludendorff staged a Putsch while I was in Munich. *A* wrote to me that she would never stay with *o* if I would be more patient. Primo de Rivera came to power while I thought of *a*."[11] One could cite many confessions of this sort relating to Marcuse's private and erotic life or the life he would like his reader to believe he had led (Cf., 97).

Evidently, Marcuse's younger years were not only spent under the sign of eros. There were other concerns which preoccupied him, foremost among them the Berlin theatre and his worship of the director Leopold Jessner, as well as the beginning of his career as a journalist and theatre critic (53-55). His employment as theatre critic in Frankfurt by the *Frankfurt Generalanzeiger* ended in 1929 with his dismissal from the paper because of internal politics, which he relates in the same almost ironic fashion as he recounts other moments in his personal life. 1929, the year of Marcuse's private defeat, was also the year of black Friday, the great stock market crash in New York. It was the year in which Stresemann died, Heinrich Himmler became Reichsführer of the SS; Trotzki was exiled from Russia. The self-styled egotist, Marcuse muses: "I am very flattered that I had such an impressive background for my private defeat."[12]

He states: "I was never influenced by ideas, only by human beings....Philosophy was for me always the history of humans, never the history of ideas."[13] In its exaggerated and almost solipsistic fixation on the individual, Marcuse's text reflects the influence of Stirner; in its combative and militant tone, it speaks of the impact of Nietzsche. To be sure, in availing himself of Nietzsche's lethal hammer, Marcuse attempts to demythologize such venerable concepts of the Left as alienation and world history (35). Marcuse presents his life as an education in pessimism, disillusionment and skepticism, which, in his view, is the only possible conclusion to be drawn from the political history of the 20th century: "Whoever has lived through this century, and who remembers only a little, and has not become a skeptic, cannot be helped."[14] Marcuse's observation refers specifically to the deception and false promises of the ideological movements in the 20th century, to which many of his contemporaries were converted, notably to the political extremism of communism and fascism. However, his pessimism is also a result of his study and experience of history and the promise of revolutions and their actual effects on historical progress. He confesses that he too had believed in revolutions until he realized that they were, in fact, ineffecutal in truly solving social and political problems: "The American Revolution taught me this, before that the French Revolution, and later the Russian Revolution....We have become accustomed to rely on world history...but we cannot rely on world history for the simple reason that it does not exist."[15] Marcuse's negation of world history, let alone of revolutions as the motor of historical progress, is directed at Hegel (376-377). It is also symptomatic of his own development leading to disillusionment with the notion of progress and, as he sees it, to his emancipation from the idealistic illusions of intellectuals who confuse the ideal and the real.

He observes of France "la douce France," that she had been his "distant beloved..., until I came to France in 1933 as a German emigrant and had to live there every day....and then suddenly it looked completely different....Then I came to America, the land of Jefferson's speeches, of Walt Whitman, of the German American enthusiast of 1848, Carl Schurz—and I was enlightened to the fact that this country is not at all a copy of the preamble of the declaration of independence, which was not its fault, but rather my illusion."[16] As presented in *Mein zwanzigstes Jahrhundert*, Marcuse's education demonstrates that the individual can never rely on the promises of ideologies, history and nations; his sole refuge is the self and the private realm. Marcuse's text can be read as both a defense of individuality, and as an attack on Hegel and Marx. In essence, Marcuse accuses both of an insidious campaign against the sanctity of the individual.

PART III

WITNESS AND VICTIM: THE AUTOBIOGRAPHICAL TEXT AS INDICTMENT

5

Lion Feuchtwanger's
Unholdes Frankreich:
Discovering the Devil in France

While Marcuse recalls his disillusionment with France and America, he does not indict these countries on moral grounds. However, this is exactly what authors such as Lion Feuchtwanger and Hans Marchwitza did, who experienced or claimed to have experienced far greater evils in those countries than Marcuse ever did. To quote from Feuchtwanger's *Unholdes Frankreich*: "Dr. F.....made a great accusatory speech. He pointed out that France had promised us hospitality....that he and...other internees had volunteered for the French Army....We had all proved that we were ready to lay down our lives in the fight against Hitler; but ... we refused to die as the victims of an inane French Officialdom."[1] Lion Feuchtwanger's recollection, however accurate, of the confrontation between Dr. F. and the French Commandant of the internment camp in Les Milles reflects the purpose of his text: the moral indictment of French authorities charged in 1940 with the internment, care and protection of German-speaking exiles and Germans working in France.

Unholdes Frankreich accuses French officials of complicity in the collapse and surrender of France: "French officals...were corrupt and inefficient. Their indolence, their corruptibility, their love of empty routine were among the causes which led to France's collapse."[2] *Unholdes Frankreich* is equally an indictment of the French for interning the exiles, many of whom were known anti-Fascists, under the pretense of military security: "We had been interned...to provide the population with a spectacle. They wanted to divert the people's attention from those who were really guilty of France's failures and who could not be brought to book."[3] At yet another point, Feuchtwanger writes: "We had been compelled to take part in this war, bound, imprisoned, impotent victims of an unreasonable, if not malign military clique."[4]

Feuchtwanger's text presents, above all, the proposition that the French were, in fact, not defeated by the Germans but by themselves, by their incompetence,[5] as well as by French Fascists who had worked hand in glove with the Nazis, and who, similar to Fascists in other countries, had been willing to sacrifice their country at the altar of fascism (206-207). For Feuchtwanger the defeat of France was even more bitter and disillusioning in light of the fact that it was not simply France's war against Germany, but the war of the anti-Fascist resistance against the Nazis: "This war was our war. Had we lost it? We had not lost it. The French Fascists had surrendered their land to our enemy."[6]

Written as an autobiographical report, *Unholdes Frankreich* recreates Feuchtwanger's imprisonment in Les Milles in 1940 and his escape in the same year from the camp at Nîmes. His text presents the autobiographical act as an act of accusation. The autobiographical reconstruction and interpretation of past experience, which in the writing of a life-story often culminates in self-discovery, takes on a decidedly different function in Feuchtwanger's text, namely to morally indict French officials for the abuse and imperilment of himself and thousands of others. In his work the recreation of past experience is tantamount to the re-discovery of the corruptibility, indifference and incompetence of French officialdom, which appears in his account in the trappings of a friendly, but potentially deadly devil: "The devil in France was a friendly well mannered devil. His devilishness came out in his polite indifference, his Je-m'en foutismus, in his slovenliness, his bureaucratic slowness....The fact that he was such a kind was worse than if he had been cruel and wicked. It would have been easier to fight cruelty and malice than red tape and slovenliness."[7] The potential deadliness of Feuchtwanger's devil is recreated in a variety of ways: Feuchtwanger recalls in particular the unsafe billeting of the prisoners in a brick factory, highly vulnerable to German air attacks (124) and the total lack of hygienic precautions in the camp at les Milles. The greatest danger and fear remembered by Feuchtwanger was that he would eventually fall into the hands of the Nazis, a fear that would lead other writers interned with Feuchtwanger to suicide, including the prominent Expressionist dramatist, Walter Hasenclever. Clearly, the danger of becoming the prisoner of the Germans was magnified a hundred fold after the collapse of France and the signing of an armistice with the Germans in June of 1940, particularly in view of clause nineteen of the armistice, stating that the French had to hand over to "the Nazis all those Germans which they asked for."[8]

Feuchtwanger recreates his discovery of the devil on different levels and in different contexts, not lastly in the context of the absurd, of the world turned upside down, of the reversal of the anticipated, expected and logical: "Not only did the French refuse any kind of collaboration on the part of us German anti-fascists, they even went so far as to imprison us."[9] In recreating the world turned upside down, Feuchtwanger recalls the fate of French Foreign Legionnaires, who, because of their central European origins were, according to Feuchtwanger, also interned: "Many of them had fought in French battles, many had lost an arm or leg in the cause of France. Almost all of them had military decorations....Even the guards were indignant that France should reward them in this way for services rendered."[10] Feuchtwanger returns repeatedly to the pitiful picture of the Legionnaires,[11] once the victors of the very Arabs who now served at the request of French commanders as their guards (109-110). Such reversals of the expected, the logical and the just, become in Feuchtwanger's memories the rule of an absurd world, in which, for instance, — air raid trenches were routinely dug and then refilled: "The wearisome labour, the senseless digging-up of the ground and filling of it again was an apt parable of our whole senseless, jeopardized existence."[12] Feuchtwanger's text often reads as series of absurd acts and grotesque misunderstandings on the part of the French, including his recreation of the prisoners' flight from Les Milles on a French train. The train seemed to always be moving back and forward, and it moved invariably too slow and in the wrong direction. In the end, French authorities had the train avoid the port city of Bayonne, a possible escape route, out of fear of encountering the Germans. They would later learn, according to Feuchtwanger, that the Germans had not been in Bayonne at all (202).

He and his fellow prisoners were, Feuchtwanger relates, "one vast homogenous horde, tattered, filthy and demoralized."[13] Feuchtwanger's narrative oscillates between "we" the prisoners and victims to the individual fate of "I" Lion Feuchtwanger, the writer whose books had denigrated Nazi barbarity and who now was imprisoned as a possible sympathizer and abettor of the Nazis:" Now at this very moment, while you lie here, I told myself, people all over the world are sitting reading your books about Nazi barbarity; rage wells up in their hearts at the thought of it, but you lie here miserably imprisoned as being unworthy of humanity, suspected of being an aider and abettor of that barbarity."[14] Feuchtwanger's days of imprisonment are recalled, in part, as the waiting in endless lines for the barest essentials: "Even now when I think of how I stood and waited in those queues a feeling of disgust, of sadness, of indignation, of utter humiliation overwhelms me."[15] To remember the queues in front of the latrines in Les Milles is equally to remember the absence of adequate water and any sort of sanitation, it is to recall days, weeks in filth: "There was no water; you could not escape from the filth and from the dense swarms of flies."[16]

The memory of filth and excrement inside the brick factory and outside in the yard is central to Feuchtwanger's reconstruction of his days in the camp at Les Milles: "At night the passage leading from the second floor to the floors below was kept locked....So people on the second floor relieved nature just where they happened to be; the urine and excrement dropped down on to us in the darkness."[17]　In addition to these images of filth and excrement, Feuchtwanger's memories include the battle against foraging rats, and the fear of becoming ill, of being sent to a French hospital, sites, in Feuchtwanger's memory, of dirt and slovenliness (106).

The most immediate privation for him was time and privacy, both of which he needed to write: "I am a slow worker, but had I been able to use for my work the time I have spent in offices and barrack-yards in futile waiting, I could have written two more books."[18] ".....The hardest thing to bear in this camp was to me the fact that one was never able to be alone, that always, day and night, during the performance of any function, eating, sleeping and relieving oneself, there were hundreds of people around one."[19] At one point he refers to the German philosopher, Theodor Lessing, an early victim of the Nazis, who had written that "to write history was to give meaning to the meaningless" ("Geschichte ist die Sinngebung des Sinnlosen", 18-19). The writing of *Unholdes Frankreich* was, in part, an attempt to give meaning to what appeared to Feuchtwanger to be an absurd time and chapter in his life, filled with senseless activities and events. While Feuchtwanger's text can be read as an indictment of the French, it can, equally be read as a warning to its first readers, the Americans, that Fascists everywhere recognize only one allegiance: the allegiance to fascism. At the same time, Feuchtwanger's text reiterates at several points that the war against fascism can be won; a text that conjures up images not of the Germans defeating the French, but images of self-destruction, of the suicide of France.

At the outset of *Unholdes Frankreich* Feuchtwanger speaks of the conjuring up of the images and events of the camps. In so doing, he emphasizes what he terms the "truth" of his accounts: "I shall confine myself to describing what I experienced as honestly, that is to say, as subjectively, as possible, without making any claims to be objective."[20] Feuchtwanger's ruminations on what he perceives as "subjective truth" are,[21] in part, linked to the fact that Feuchtwanger wrote *Unholdes Frankreich* in New York without any notes concerning his confinement, relying completely on the vagaries and capriciousness of memory: "...I think capriciousness of... memory is of advantage to a writer. It compels him to that absolute honesty which is an essential condition of all writing, it forces him to communicate only such visions which are really his visions....I am obliged because of the loss of my notes to present a picture, not crude photographic reality."[22]

6

Hans Marchwitza's *In Amerika*: The Demon Capitalism and the Land of Limited Opportunities

The question, of course, is at what point memory in all its subjectivity is compromised by the dictates of political expediency or ideology. This question is of particular relevance in the case of the Communist proletarian writer, Hans Marchwitza. Similar to Feuchtwanger, Marchwitza was also interned in Les Milles and in Nîmes; his experience in those camps takes up only a small part of his autobiograhical report *In Frankreich* (1949) which, while at points critical of the French, can in no way be read as Feuchtwanger's text can — as a moral indictment of France. Still, Marchwitza would avail himself once again of autobiography to indict the United States, the country of his final exile.

It has been argued that autobiography invariably involves a collusion of the present and the past; its significance is more truly understood as the revelation of the present situation of the autobiographer than as the uncovering of his or her past. In brief, memory and imagination shape the presentation of past experiences to serve the needs of a present consciousness (Pascal, 11; Eaken, 56). Such reflections are particularly relevant for Marchwitza's autobiographical report of his experiences in exile in New York. Although no one can deny that Marchwitza was a committed Communist at the time of his exile in 1941 to the United States, his text appeared at the height of the Cold War, at a time when America had been denigrated for years by Communist propaganda. Published in 1961 in the then German Democratic Republic, the year in which the "Berlin Wall" was built, the text was slated first and foremost for internal consumption, as a tool of political enlightenment and indoctrination, designed to instruct the East German reader as to the "true" nature of America, which, in Marchwitza's presentation emerges not as a land of prosperity and opportunities but as a country of hollow promises and harsh social realities. Marchwitza's *In Amerika* takes its place among the literary works of the former German Democratic Republic reflecting the Communist party's stand on life in the United States.[1]

Marchwitza's text represents not only the collusion of the past and present, but more precisely the collusion of memory and propaganda, creating a text with a specific political aim: the demonization of America, remembered by Marchwitza as the fortress of capitalism and as a land of decidedly limited opportunities for workers. Therefore, *In Amerika* is as much a reflection of current Communist propaganda as it is a record of Marchwitza's experiences in New York. Moreover, Marchwitza's text is equally an autobiographical text with fictional antecedents. The cold, intimidating and ruthlessly competitive world portrayed in Franz Kafka's *Amerika*, in which speed and time play crucial roles in the game of survival, is taken to new extremes in Marchwitza's text.[2] Upon his arrival in New York harbor, Kafka's Karl Rossmann experiences the statue of liberty as a lady holding an upturned sword in an almost threatening gesture, while the free winds of heaven ironically circle about her. Marchwitza's own memories of his arrival in New York equally place the statue of liberty in an ironic and threatening context.[3] The smile and promise of Lady Liberty is belied and contradicted by the cold and menacing concrete towers of New York City, rising above and beyond the symbol of freedom. Each tower looms in Marchwitza's memory as a citadel of the demon money, which transformed the smile of the Statue of Liberty into a mockery of the promise it symbolized (*In Amerika*, 298).

Marchwitza's text also evokes associations with Upton Sinclair's *The Jungle*. The site of the exploitation of the worker has shifted from the stinking and dangerous slaughter houses of Chicago to the desolate construction sites in and around the city of New York. *In Amerika* tells the story of Marchwitza as witness to and victim of a predatory, merciless, and socially unjust society. It is a society permeated with racism, insecurity and fear, the fear of losing one's job and of poverty, and thus of becoming one of the hundreds of the homeless populating the streets of New York City (303). At the same time, to remember America is to conjure up images of the true and implacable enemy, namely the captains of capitalism, the Morgans and Rockefellers. Marchwitza's memory of the barbarity of fascism pales before the specter of capitalism, a mark of his text revealing, on the one hand, the Marxist notion that fascism is but an extreme form of capitalism, and on the other, the text as propaganda, decrying and denigrating the West.

In his indictment of America Marchwitza's strategy is to demythologize and to demonize, to lay bare America's hollow promises, to unmask the demon, America; to reveal and deconstruct the central myths underpinning American ideology. He attacks the notion of America as a melting pot of nationalities and races, a country accepting people regardless of race and origin and integrating them into American society: "I heard a couple of times New York called a melting pot. What they really meant was that here in the bubbling boiler refugees from all over the world, hoping for salvation, were remelted like plunder and raw material to become what they were really wanted for in New York: cheap willing slaves and fools."[4] Marchwitza presents his own experiences in New York as a physical and psychological test, a test as to whether a Communist would be broken in body and mind by the yoke of capitalism: "These are tests, it is America ...this icy, heartless America."[5] Marchwitza's experiences constitute a microcosm of the larger story of the exploited and suffering workers in New York. It is true that for him, who spoke very little English, and who was fifty when he arrived in America, opportunities were plainly limited. We witness Marchwitza, the painter and carpenter's apprentice, the cement mixer, the construction and demolition worker. If we wish to believe Marchwitza, such jobs could, in the exploitative environment of America, have very well cost him his life. Thus, the memory of Marchwitza's putative poisoning as a painter's apprentice is presented as evidence of the exploitation and abuse of the worker in a land of false promises and deception: "I lay in bed for almost fourteen days with cramps and completely exhausted. I had time to think about America whose 'unlimited opportunities' I believed to have learned enough about."[6]

Clearly, one of Marchwitza's strategies in reconstructing his experiences in America was to deter the interest of East Germans in America. Stories of physical pain and torment, of exploitative and inhuman working conditions are hallmarks of Marchwitza's text. The demythologizing of the land of unlimited opportunities occurs in direct relation to the alleged sufferings of the autobiographer, Marchwitza. He recalls, for example, injuries and pain which he supposedly suffered while scraping and sanding as a painter's apprentice: "When I put my hands into the hot soda water my eyes filled with tears from the pain. While I scrubbed, I felt as if I were scouring pain tormented hands over glowing coals. Luckily, I found an old burlap bag to put under my knees in which there seemed since yesterday to be burning thorns."[7] The reconstruction of such memories evidently serves the purpose of pointing out the contradiction between the mythical America of "unlimited opportunities" and the actual, allegedly pitiful situation of the American worker.

Marchwitza's self-representation as an exploited and tormented worker culminates in the image of himself as a human machine: "Yes, we are in America...here you yourself have to do the work of a machine."[8] This observation occurs in Marchwitza's memory of straightening iron girders by hand: "...bending, lifting and hammering...until several times I sank completely out of breath to the floor to rest a few minutes."[9] The image of the worker as a machine is central to Marchwitza's indictment of America: "Yes, that's America! Here you have to leave your feelings outside....and become a lever or a swinging crane."[10] In these memories the worker appears ultimately as a robot in a society in which human dignity and self-respect have been replaced by economic slavery (336, 386).

The focus of Marchwitza's narrative frequently shifts from recounting his own sufferings to those of others, particularly the fates of earlier German immigrants. These accounts serve, in turn, to reinforce the credibility and authenticity of Marchwitza's personal afflictions: "A dishwasher who did not become a millionare" ("Ein Tellerwäscher, der kein Millionär wurde," 394) is the programmatic title of a chapter treating the alleged fate of an earlier immigrant. Be it the story of the toiling dishwasher or that of the elderly pianist, who must conceal her age in order to keep her job, the lesson is always the same. The promise of security and freedom in America is a deception: "I thought of the dishwasher...who similar to the artist, had hoped to become a human being in...America and how with the first breath of 'golden freedom' deception began to dig their grave."[11] Marchwitza's strategy to demythologize America is all encompassing. Witness Marchwitza's accounts of the self-destruction of America's capitalists and investors: "I stood in the midst of the giant concrete towers....The camp of money and stock battles, speculation, deceit, the source of insanity and innumerable murders and suicides."[12] America emerges in such lines as a nightmare, if not as a form of hell.

In Marchwitza's reconstruction of his years in American exile as a Communist and an outsider he must necessarily remember the other outsiders of America, notably America's blacks, with whom he readily identifies The proletarian writer and Communist was for the Capitalist rulers of Germany, in Marchwitza's words, little more than a black: "I had also been a black and had been treated with the same contempt."[13] Central to Marchwitza's presentation of Black America is the indictment of America's hypocrisy, racism and social injustice. Black men emerge in this text as the unsung heroes of World War II: "It was not these black men who had won the victories in North Africa and Italy and on the islands. America had won them. The gloomy cement towers of America, the busy banks and the full vaults of America had won them."[14] Marchwitza presents his memory of the war and America's role in the war as a memory of history repeating itself. The exploited proletariat was sent out to protect the nation's wealth, in which it will never share. In the end, both poor whites and blacks, who are the victims of racism and oppression by the ruling class, are condemned to fight the wars of racist and capitalist America: "March black, march white

nigger, the fatherland of injustice, the fatherland of slavehold-
ers has to be defended, it needs space for expansion."[15]
Clearly, these lines are not only evoked by memory, but by the
Communist need to denounce America for its purported insatiable quest for economic and political dominance, not to mention its encirclement of the Communist East. There are different levels and functions of memory and remembering in
Marchwitza's text. In the broadest sense the text remembers
the call to world revolution against international capitalism,
particularly in its American version. In this context Marchwitza conjures up memories of paintings in a friend's apart-
ment, representing a kind of primeval forest, wherein a giant
was raging, swinging a powerful ax. This giant was, according
to Marchwitza, the American worker who had a lot to clear in
the wilderness of America (306). Clearly, such memories are
inextricably linked to a Communist agenda of revolutionary
politics. Indeed, Marchwitza's text represents a blatant example, of reading and filtering memory through the glass and
screen of ideology.

PART IV

FOREGROUNDING THE SELF AS THE OTHER: STORIES OF SHYLOCK AND AMAZONS, AND THE PERENNIAL OUTSIDER

7

Fritz Kortner's *Aller Tage Abend*: Self-Discovery as the Discovery of the Other or a Life and Career as Shylock

The autobiographies of the exiles present not only the story of the politically persecuted, but even more so that of the racially persecuted exile. Some exiles were both left-wing intellectuals and assimilated Jews. One thinks of such figures as Toni Sender, Ernst Toller, Alfred Döblin, Lion Feuchtwanger, Ludwig Marcuse, Robert Neumann, Manès Sperber, and Stephan Heym, to name but a few. The texts written by Jewish exiles, however assimilated, may contain vivid memories of discrimination, harassment and persecution, but also the problem of alienation from one's Jewish roots, the desire to shed and conceal one's Jewishness, often initiating the process of acculturation and assimilation.[1] Many of these recollections deal with childhood in Germany and Austria years before the advent of Nazism,[2] others are situated in the period of exile. The specter and realities of anti-Semitism could be discovered thousands of miles away from Nazi Germany, even in mines and pits of Bolivia and Chile.[3] Other texts look back, recounting the lives of friends and relatives who stayed behind to become victims of the camps.[4]

The life-story of the Jewish exile may be devoted to recreating a life overshadowed and forever threatened by anti-Semitism. Fritz Kortner's *Aller Tage Abend* (1969) is a text preoccupied with the problematics of persecution, as well as with Kortner's memory of his own long and indefatigable struggle against anti-Semitism, which, according to Kortner, followed upon his earlier years of acculturation and assimilation in Austria and Germany. More importantly, Kortner's text attempts to deal with the changing perceptions of the self and the problematics of identity, molded by the intersection of the self and the anti-Semitic world around the self.

The writing of autobiography is often viewed as an act of self-discovery. Certainly, this holds true of Kortner's *Aller Tage Abend* whose author, in the act of remembering, recreates the contours and turning points of a life, first spent fleeing but ultimately combatting anti-Semitism; first rejecting, yet finally accepting Jewish identity. The clarity Kortner attains concerning his life centers on an identity forsaken and yet reclaimed, the clarity about a life threatened yet redeemed; still a life which, from Kortner's perspective, is, similar to the lives of all Jews, perennially threatened: "We whose lives are always threatened."[5] At the same time, however, Kortner's text relates self-discovery in the context of Kortner's childhood and youth in an anti-Semitic world. The intersection of the self in Kortner's text and the world about the self is the story of self-discovery, the discovery of one's otherness, of one's Jewishness, of the Jew's maligned status as an outsider, who must exist under the specter and threat of abuse and genocide.

Kortner's childhood played out before the background of the anti-Semitic campaigns and propaganda then prevalent at the turn of the century in the Vienna of Karl Lueger, who in his successful bid in 1897 for the office of mayor of Vienna had exploited and fueled anti-Semitism. It was the Vienna where a few years later Adolf Hitler would receive much of his instruction in anti-Semitism, and from which he would embark on a campaign of hate and genocide, ultimately culminating in the Holocaust. Kortner's memories of his early life in Vienna extend from the physical brutalization of a child to the psychological abuse of a young actor; and they tell of his own early childhood victimization at the hands of anti-Semitic propaganda.

Thus, Kortner's childhood is not recalled and recreated as a time of security and innocence, but as a time of fear and trauma. For Kortner remembering and recreating a Jewish boy's childhood in Vienna is to recall the fear of being recognized as a Jew, of being an object of verbal and physical abuse.

The conjuring up of such memories is to speak at once of abuse and discovery, the abuse of a Jewish child and the discovery of oneself as "the Other": "I may have been five or six years old, when one day as I was sitting dreamily in front of my father's store...two rogues appeared. They looked huge to me and horrible. One of the huns bent down to me...I was paralyzed by fright...his fingers grasped my hair close to my ears, where it is the most painful, twisted them, pulled me up by the hair until I stood. Then the other slugged...the Jewish boy in the face. I screamed from fear and pain."[6] Although Kortner recalls that he was rescued by his father from this "nightmarish terror" ("alptraumhaften Schreckenfall," Ibid), the experience and its memory play a pivotal role in the story of his self-discovery, the discovery of oneself as the "Other," as the Jew in the mirror of anti-Semitic hate.

Recreated with all the trappings of a nightmare and trauma this "Kindheitsschreck" (47), is also interpreted by Kortner as a turning point in the psychological development of a child. It marks the transformation of Kortner from a dreamy and sleepy boy ("verschalfenen Buben") into a terrified and frightened one ("aufgeschreckte(n) und entsetzte(n) Junge(n)", 329); It is recalled by Kortner as his first deep wounding at the hands of anti-Semitism (47). The discovery of oneself as "the Other," as the Jew, is synonymous with the discovery of the hostile and threatening world about one. It leads, in Kortner's case, first to a child's escape into the security of Judaic belief, the mysticism of the bible (329), an escape culminating in visions of the self as a Rabbi, praying against the sinfulness of the world, and against the perpetrators and agents of violence.

The memory of the persecution and brutalization of a Jewish child in Vienna at the turn of the century transcends individual experience. It is part of a collective memory of the beginnings of a development in the late 19th and 20th century, namely the radicalization of anti-Semitism,[7] culminating in the persecution and murder of the Jews in the Third Reich, a development whose early manifestation in Austria shattered Kortner's world of childhood dreams, illusions and innocence (46). Memories of brutalization in the recreation of Kortner's childhood are followed by the memory of his victimization at the hands of anti-Semitic propaganda, to his own early suspicion and fear of Jews as the ritual murderers of Christians (22). As he recreates his childhood, it appears as a series of traumatic encounters with the world about him; traumas undercutting his sense of security and identity, leading to Kortner's early estrangement from his immediate family, to the anxiety and fear that his own father was a ritual murderer, to the fear that family meals contained the blood of Christians: "And one day as red beets were being served I fell unconscious."[8] Intimidation, fear, pain, trauma, and suspicion are intertwined in Kortner's memories of his early childhood, creating the image of a child as the victim of psychological torments and physical abuse.

The memory and recreation of Kortner's childhood and youth in Vienna reflects not only the continuing self-discovery of his status and fate as an outsider but also his attempts to overcome that status and image. To remember such attempts, is to recreate the story of the self as a social underdog and outsider, embracing such sports as soccer as the key to acceptance and reward. For Kortner it was the specific linking of success in soccer with the shedding of his otherness. Remembering the shooting of each goal in soccer is the memory of an illusion of acceptance in the Christian world about him (329), an illusion shattered at the ending of each game and the resumption of anti-Semitic slurs, the return of Kortner's identity not as a valued soccer player, but as a Jew and thus an outsider, an object of ridicule, scorn and abuse.

Moreover, the recreation of his early years in Vienna involve, for Kortner, continuing changes in the perception of self. As an acting student in Vienna, he discovers his specific Jewish appearance, as mirrored through the glass of anti-Semitism. Instruction in acting would become for Kortner, above all, instruction in his Jewish physiognomy, in his specific ugliness, remembered as the basis and justification for the rejection of his wish to play the role of Melchthal in Schiller's *Wilhelm Tell*. Julius Meixner told him: "With that face you can never play Melchthal, with that face you should not be in the theatre at all. In a business or a bank'(your face) will not be a problem at all."[9] These words from an anti-Semite were,

Kortner recalls, extremely painful, leaving an indelible imprint on the mind of the boy; an almost irreversible self-image as the "ugly one" (ibid). Of course, such memories evoke equally the envied and maligned image of the Jew as merchant and money lender, the religiously and socially sanctioned professions for the Jew for centuries. Kortner's acting teacher in Vienna is remembered and portrayed by him as the detractor of Kortner's facial features, and as the destroyer of Kortner's self-confidence, who availed himself of an infamous repertoire of anti-Semitic slurs: "I have little to thank Meixner...as an actor, but (a great deal) for the knowledge of my ugliness which is (so) difficult to overcome."[10]

The perception of the self in the mirror of anti-Semitism, as presented in Kortner's text, is also the perception of one's ugliness and inferiority. The overcoming of those perceptions only occurs in Kortner's reconstruction of his life during his exile in America and during his later journeys to Israel. (Cf. 292). In his childhood and youth, he suffered, as he sees it, not only physical and psychological abuse, and acquired feelings of inferiority and rejection, but also became estranged from his Jewish identity. He was enamored by one of the most vociferous prophets of Jewish self-hate,[11] namely Karl Kraus and his literary campaigns against Viennese Jewry and against the father of Zionism, Theodor Herzl: "Why, as a young man, did I so uncritically read and agree with these anti-Jewish pamphlets?"[12] Moreover, Kortner claims to have decided at age fifteen to either avoid or to conceal all external signs of being a Jew, a decision linked to earlier abuse, but also to his hope of becoming a successful actor (16).

Yet, *Aller Tage Abend* plays back not only the discovery of the self in the mirror of anti-Semitism, but also the discovery of one's loss of Jewish identity and solidarity with fellow Jews. Kortner situates that discovery in the ghettos of Poland and Russia at the time of his journey in 1911 with the theatre of Max Reinhardt to Eastern Europe. As the memory of Russia unfolds, it does so first as the memory of discovering recent pogroms: "I stood there dismayed. Shy and alone I snuck into the ghetto. I had seen the first (ghetto) in Warsaw. I was not overwhelmed by empathy and compassion as I expected, and

as I had felt it was my duty to be."[13] Kortner's confrontation
with the reality of the pogroms and his discovery of the still
living Jews in the ghettos of the East are recreated as moments
of self-recognition: "My assimilation had taken me too far
from them. I was a world away from the Ghetto and its cus-
toms."[14] Above all, Kortner was both terrified by the idea of
belonging completely to Judaism and alienated from its modern version and expression in Zionism (112). The recreation
of such scenes of recognition are situated before World War I,
at a time when Kortner's life, as he depicts it, reflected an
estrangement and flight from Jewish identity and the call of
Zionism. Moreover, the recreation of such scenes from his life
mirror the beginnings of Kortner's rediscovery of anti-
Semitism in its most brutal and inhuman form, in the form of
horrors visited upon Jews.

Kortner recreates his life following World War I as a return
to and deepening of his Jewish identity, culminating in the
beginnings of his struggle against anti-Semitism, first carried
out through the medium of the stage and later in film. His
life-story now becomes the story of the discovery of "the
Other" in the theatre and in film, and of his identification
with Jewish characters. Kortner as Shylock, as Professor Bernhardi, as Dreyfus, as the young rebel, Friedrich, in Ernst
Toller's *Die Verwandlung* are among the more vividly recalled
Jewish figures, for whose portrayal Kortner would become at
once celebrated and vilified. He writes of playing Friedrich in
Toller's drama: "What I played at that time was myself; a
young German Jew and rebel, in conflict with the world about
him."[15] The conflict for which Kortner would become particularly known and vilified was the conflict of the Jewish actor
with the anti-Semitic world about him, and specifically Kortner's attempts to present the Jew as victim. Kortner's portrayal of such figures constitutes not only the story of the
identification of the self with the role it is acting, but also of
deconstructing received interpretations of figures, as in his
now famous rendering of Shylock.

Remembering his interpretation of Shylock in Jürgen
Fehling's 1927 production of the *Merchant of Venice* he writes:
"I was eager to play a Shylock, who, having been treated

inhumanly by the Christian world about him, becomes (himself) inhuman...I wanted to unmask Christian hate and reveal a false morality."[16]   Kortner's role as Shylock in Fehling's production of the *Merchant of Venice* is recalled as provoking a barrage of invectives from such Nazi papers as "Der Stürmer" (242).   In the eyes of anti-Semites, foremost among them, the Nazis, Kortner's interpretation of Shylock as victim was symptomatic of his Jewish aggressiveness, and of the transformation of the German theatre into a "Jewish" institution.[17]   Clearly, it won him the unremitting hate of anti-Semites, leading to threats of murder.[18]   Indeed, from the Nazi perspective the demise of the aggressive Kortner was particularly desireable (268).

The tension in Kortner's text, particularly in his recreation of his life and career between 1919 and 1933 springs from his memory of success as a Jewish actor, fighting for the cause of the oppressed and threatened Jew and the ever-threatening waves of anti-Semitism about him.   To remember the invectives of the Nazi press is to recall the accusations against Kortner as a rapist of Christian women; it is to recall slander and intimidation, but above all, it is to remember the relentless invention of the Jew as "the Other," as the pariah, the outcast, as the morally dubious. The memory and the reconstruction of the reception of Kortner's roles as Shylock, Dreyfus and Professor Bernhardi is at once the memory of the divisions in German society; the memory of supporters and detractors, defenders and persecutors. It is a memory which gives way to that of the inexorable victory of anti-Semitism in the guise of Nazism.

The defeat and destruction of Nazi Germany, and particularly the founding of the state of Israel are remembered by Kortner as the return of his trust in historical progress and life: "My trust in life is (inextricably) linked to this symbol of justice."[19] Still, remembering and recreating one's career as a campaign against anti-Semitism does not end in Kortner's text with the destruction of the Third Reich. Kortner's memory of his return to Europe following World War II and his work as a director in Germany is synonymous with the resumption of that struggle, reflected in his plans to stage such plays as *Die*

Affäre Dreyfus.   At the same time, it is synonymous with the rediscovery of anti-Semitism in the theatre, particularly in the case of actors unwilling to play the role of the Jew, Dreyfus (202).   Be it the staging of *Die Affäre Dreyfus* or Bernhard Shaw's *Androcles and the Lion*, Kortner recreates each within the context of the struggle against anti-Semitism (290).   Still, Kortner's text is not only one of rememberance but also of anticipation of the continuing persecution of the Jews (339).   Thus, *Aller Tage Abend* is the story of the autobiographer as "the Other," the outsider, as a representative figure of the perennially threatened race: "We who were already threatened in our youth; we who were chosen for persecution, we who are always threatened."[20]

8

Toni Sender's *Autobiographie einer deutschen Rebellin*: Valorizing Her Quest for Independence, Her Politics and Disease

Autobiographie einer deutschen Rebellin presents the first half of Toni Sender's life, spanning the years 1888 to 1935. It first appeared in English in 1939 in New York under the title *Autobiography of a German Rebel*. The title may have been influenced by Angelica Balabanova's autobiography, *My Life as a Rebel*, published a year earlier in English translation in New York.[1] Sender structures her narrative around her quest for independence and her career as a political activist and left-wing politician, as well as around her recurring bouts with tuberculosis. Her text situates Sender in what has come to be known as the "individualist feminist tradition", celebrating "the quest for personal independence in all aspects of life, while...deprecating or dismissing as insignificant all socially defined roles..." (Offen, 136). Moreover, much of Sender's story takes place inside traditional male narratives of independence, heroism, self-sufficiency, isolation, power, purpose and the flight from domesticating conventionality.[2] As for Sender's self-representation as a rebel, it is linked to the story of her life as a series of rebellions, first carried out against her orthodox Jewish family, subsequently against the patriarchal values and war policies of Imperial Germany, and ultimately against Nazi intimidation on the eve of the Third Reich.

Central to Sender's self-representation as a rebel is the story of her quest for independence and self-realization, whose beginnings Sender situates in her childhood. She recalls her early urge to be free and independent of her parents and of her inner revolt against parental authority, and the unquestioning obedience demanded by her parents. This revolt first manifested itself in a child's silence and reticence: "You almost never talked."[3] Her seemingly taciturn nature is presented as symptomatic of her persistent inner rebellion against "the gloomy days of submission and obedience,"[4] which in Sender's text encompasses both her childhood and her early youth, at home and in school: "...few of my teachers had any idea of the force of the inner-rebellion that I was keeping down."[5] Yet, Sender does not characterize all schools as institutions of oppression; for some institutions were to her synonymous with distance and independence from parental authority, and above all, they held the promise of economic independence. Says Sender of her early studies at a business school in Frankfurt: "I confess that I had no idea what sort of calling I was really choosing. ....The only factor that counted was that within two years I should no longer be dependent upon my family."[6]

In recalling and reinventing her urge to be independent of others, Sender includes male friends and lovers. Sender's recollection of her refusal to marry a fellow French Socialist shortly before World War I is a case in point. She had left Imperial Germany in 1910, a country "...where I had suffered such restraints on my independence."[7] For the next four years she would work and study in Paris. And there, she felt "for the first time in my life at home!"[8] It was to be the city where she spent "....the most active and wonderful time of my life."[9] Still, in Sender's recollection of her refusal to enter a marriage which would have allowed her to remain in Paris during World War I, her commitment to personal independence is presented as the sole touchstone and arbiter of her actions: "Under the circumstances, I was afraid that marriage would make me too dependent on my friend, economically and otherwise. I knew myself well enough to realize that it might be too severe a strain on my strong sense of independence and might destroy the harmony we had enjoyed together."[10]

The quest for independence, be it from parents, friends or lovers is central in the unfolding story of Sender's life. At almost any given point in her text, Sender returns to depictions of her urge to be independent of others, both materially and emotionally, in both her private and public life (Cf. 176, 179, 235). Of course, Sender's text also presents her life-story as one of political rebellion. Sender recalls her early years in Frankfurt at the turn of the century as a period in which she became part of the emerging struggle for social justice in Germany. The image she fashions of herself in this context is both heroic and sacrificial. The first political demonstration in which Sender recalls participating was directed against the spurious and inequitable voting laws in Wilhelmian Germany. It culminated in the police beating of demonstrators, including Sender: "...A rain of blows. My back hurt terribly.... That evening remained in the memory of thousands as Frankfurt's bloody night."[11] The events of Frankfurt's "bloody night", as she recalls it, precipitated her political radicalization. She was "...driven by a compulsion stronger than myself and I had to go along the road on which I had started upon."[12] It was a compulsion that led her to join the Socialist movement in 1906, a step which she considers "a decisive moment in my life."[13] It constitutes the second turning point in her life-story, following her financial independence from her parents and her break with the stifling and oppressive life, which had been her fate as a child and young woman.

Sender recalls in detail the first important chapters in the story of her political career. We witness Sender, the antiwar activist and pacifist leader, the organizer of women's groups opposed to World War I, as an associate of such radical figures of the Left as Rosa Luxembourg and Clara Zetkin, and as an Independent Socialist and advocate of the revolution of 1918: "I wrote, I announced the success of the revolution, the establishment of a social republic. I advised the population that Workers and Soldiers Councils had been formed and now represented the supreme authority."[14] *Autobiographie einer deutschen Rebellin* presents the political figure of Toni Sender as a woman who was in constant motion, and as a story of self-sacrifice and heroism. Interwoven into the memory of political struggles and campaigns is the story of a biological struggle against tuberculosis. Sender links the inception of the disease to aspects of her character and individuality. Sender recalls a maxim she had once learned in school, which, she believes directly influenced her later conduct in social and political causes: "To do nothing half way is the way of noble minds. This admonition has accompanied me through my life and has often been an encouragement and a reminder of the high intentions with which I started."[15] This admonition plays a central role in her urge to commit herself to social causes and political crusades, often to the point of self-destruction. At such moments, memories of political rebellion and struggle give way to the memory of a biological struggle against exhaustion and disease.

Thus, to give one example, Sender appears in the early weeks of the new German Republic both as a revolutionary Socialist, and as a woman, experiencing an ominous decline in her health: "I could not withstand the drain on my strength any longer. A high fever and a severe influenza, which affected my lungs, overcame me."[16] That illness, she recalls, almost cost her her life. However, having barely regained some of her strength and still stricken with fever, she resumed her work, writing articles for the revolution "which our weekly expected of me. But the fever persisted."[17] The interplay of self-sacrifice and exhaustion, of indefatigable commitment and persistent illness, becomes yet another recurring feature in Sender's self-representation: "During all these days I had not undressed, had not slept."[18] The reference is to Sender's activities in Frankfurt during the precarious days of the Kapp Putsch in 1920, when she recalls having worked ceaselessly to keep a general strike of workers alive against the insurrectionists. Again the pattern of self-portrayal is that of commitment and self-denial, herculean tasks, and ensuing exhaustion and eventual illness.

Sender was involved in many distinct, though intersecting and interrelated movements, as feminist, pacifist, left-wing Socialist and revolutionary, as a Reichstag-deputy, internationalist and trade unionist. Sender reconstructs her unequivocal opposition to the Soviets' early attempt to dominate the World Labor Movement: "My reaction was immediate. Unacceptable! I always understood the struggle of labor as a fight for freedom, not as the submission to zealots, to some superior command in Moscow."[19] Recalling the fight to defeat the German advocates of Soviet control of the World Labor Movement, she writes, emphasizing her state of physical exhaustion: "I had not yet had a rest and needed it badly....I had to go from state to state to oppose speakers who wanted to split our party and lead it into the Communist ranks and to submission to the Moscow central committee....I was successful in many places, once having to speak for three and a half hours....It was a grand battle....and I have never regretted leading it."[20] What emerges as the cost of that battle and others is the acceleration of Sender's deteriorating state of health: "I became weaker and weaker and was sent ...to a sanatarium. It did not help much."[21] Recalling a renewed physical breakdown in 1921, she writes: "Tuberculosis of the lungs was the physician's diagnosis. I was forced into a hospital and sanatarium—first in Austria, later in Germany."[22]

Sender's early career in politics was crowned in 1920, when at the age of thirty-two she was elected as a candidate of the Independent Socialist Party to the Reichstag: "I was put at the head of the national ticket....I was to remain in the Reichstag for thirteen years."[23] The story of Sender's career in the Reichstag is also the story of her struggle for recognition as a woman in an institution dominated by men: "A woman must make a greater effort, must show more efficiency than a man in order to be recognized as an equal. Once, however, her ability is recognized and acknowledged, one can forget about difference of sex."[24] Such reflections, however candid, can be seen as symptomatic of Sender's oppression in a male dominated institution, in the arena in which she had, by her own accounts, to struggle for recognition.

As a Reichstag deputy Sender appears as a champion of free trade: "My efforts were directed toward breaking down ...custom walls by reciprocal trade treaties."[25] She characterizes herself as "the only guardian of the general and consumer interests."[26] Again this role is presented within a context of failing health: "No one was surprised in the winter of

1927 when I suffered a reappearance of tuberculosis. Again, I found myself on the magic mountain in Davos."[27] The cycle of political activism and physical breakdown becomes the dominant aspect in Sender's self-presentation. Yet, it does not deter her from conjuring up the image of herself as a "lonely warrior," who discovered during debates in the Reichstag a weakness of the so-called stronger sex. That weakness stemmed not from a lack of physical stamina, but from a lack of self-discipline: "...the representatives of the stronger sex, when the night hours approached, felt tired and unable to make any further efforts....I was never weary before the meeting was over—because during my activity in public life I had always imposed self-discipline upon myself."[28] Sender's self-image as a lonely warrior and crusader is also evoked in her recollection of her fight in 1930 in the Reichstag for reciprocal trade agreements. As Sender describes the event, she was pitted against both the extreme Left as well as the extreme Right, who directed their attacks against her: "Convinced of the soundness of my position, I persistently fought my way through."[29]

In the final pages of her text, Sender assumes the part of a fearless defender of the Weimar Republic. By 1930 almost half of the members of the Reichstag were opposed to democracy (248). As a woman, a Jew and a Social Democrat, Sender was destined for harassment at the hands of the Nazis. Recalling her first speech before the Reichstag in 1930 with the newly elected Nazi opposition, Sender writes: "I had scarcely begun to talk when a hail of interruptions—shouts, catcalls, laughter—came from the Nazis. I retorted with a violent attack on the rioters. I bitterly denounced them."[30] Sender's weekly meetings with the electorate are recreated as confrontations with the Nazis: "Since the September elections of 1930, I had to fight with the Nazis at almost every one of my meetings."[31] The Nazi campaign against Sender is remembered as a tour de force of defamation and character assassination: "In the streets and public houses they were saying that I was... a prostitute."[32] Worse yet, Sender reconstructs the final years of the Weimar Republic not only as years of defamation and character assassination by the "new

Barbarians," but as the precarious period of possible assassination. Her vivid memory of the burning of the Reichstag is linked to the escalation of Nazi terror, and above all, to the terrorization of Sender: "In Dresden they published a paper called the "Judenspiegel" ("Jews'Mirror"). The entire first page was covered with my picture and the text under it hinted that I ought to be done away with."[33] Sender's memory of her flight in 1933 from Germany to Czechoslovakia culminates in the picture of her "terrible physical and emotional collapse. I had a high fever-a relapse into my old illness."[34] While the earlier stages of Sender's illness are presented as a result of an all-consuming commitment to her work, to democracy and socialism in Germany, her relapse is remembered as the consequence of a valiant struggle against the Nazis, and the latter's relentless persecution of their foes, particularly when the foe was a Jewish woman and a socialist, who had advocated the revolution of 1918.

Sender's life, as recreated in her text, could very well have ended in the total decay and collapse of her physical and mental self. Whatever her design, she emerges from the pages of her self-portrayal as a figure oscillating between heroism and martyrdom. Her *Autobiographie einer deutschen Rebellin* contains the story of a heroic woman, struggling for equality, and defending democracy and socialism, even though her struggles bring emotional and physical deterioration, disease and the specter of death. Sender's text moves within the context of male narratives. She celebrates not only her independence as a woman, but equally women's shedding of traditional feminine roles, their break with conventionality, their assumption of traditional male roles, and even the reversal of male and female roles. Luxuriating in the memory of her refusal in 1919 to accept a traditionally feminine assignment on a committee for social problems in Frankfurt, Sender writes: "My fellow Socialists were greatly surprised when I told them...that one of the men would have to deal with matters concerning household problems, I would not do it ...."[35]

9

Hilde Spiel's *Die hellen und die finsteren Zeiten 1911-1946*: The Struggle for Self-Realization and the Crises of Multiple Identities

Breaking away from feminine domesticity and conventionality is equally the mark of Hilde Spiel's self-representation in *Die hellen und finsteren Zeiten* (1989), especially in the final chapters of her book, spanning the years 1936 to 1946, which she spent in London and to a lesser extent on the Continent, together with her first husband, the writer Peter de Mendelssohn. These final chapters of Hilde Spiel's book, which deal with her years in exile and the immediate postwar period, also pay eloquent tribute to English women and men who were active in the London Pen Club, where they assisted and helped arriving exiles from Germany, Austria and Czechoslovakia (161). Spiel's memories and images of the large and important left-wing literary scene in the Thirties in London also recreates her laudable, but often exhausting and vain attempts to help fellow writers and intellectuals to secure visas for England. The final chapters equally contain the images of an exile who is pulled inexorably by the emotional bonds to her parents and to her home, the story of Spiel's returns and forays into the Vienna of Austro-fascism before the deluge of 1938 (169/172).

Spiel's poignant, disquieting and probing account of her life in London during the *Blitz*, and of her travels to the European continent in the aftermath of World War II is designed to reflect the apparent tragedies and disharmonies in her life at that time. Her presentation of the years from 1936 to 1946 is the story of conflicting identities, a story, reinvented with the help of references to letters. Similar to the earlier chapters of *Die hellen und finsteren Zeiten*, the portrayal of Spiel's years in England unfolds as an intimate story, opening up, however selectively, a private life and world. Like Sender, Spiel also represents herself as a woman rebelling against traditional female roles, notably as she puts it, the "the cursed existence of a housewife."[1] Spiel emerges as a figure convinced by the end of the war that life was running away from her (216), and that she would not be able as a journalist and writer to take part in the intellectual renewal and rebuilding of Europe. In short, she presents herself as a woman shackled at that time by domestic and familial responsibilities.

At the same time, she also alludes to her feelings of being overshadowed by the intellectual virtuosity and acrobatics of her husband, Peter de Mendelssohn, and his circle of male writers, including Bruno Frank, Carl Zuckmayer and Robert Neumann. Theirs was a world still very much dominated by men, where men performed and women often remained silent (153). Spiel's juxtaposition of herself, her husband and his circle of friends, particularly the memory of her silence in the face of their loquaciousness and verbal acrobatics comes very close to recent feminist observations on the conservative notion of woman coexisting in a subordinated role with her male counterpart: "Dependent to his independent...encumbered to his autonomous, silent and invisible to his articulate" (Sidonie Smith, 13). Spiel's reflections on the inequalities between herself and Mendelssohn move on different levels, including also inequalities other than those that are the products of conventions in a patriarchal society. Thus, she recalls Peter de Mendelssohn's "marked linguistic talent,"[2] which made it so much easier for him than for her, to write and publish in English. The story of Hilde Spiel's and Peter de Mendelssohn's exile in London, as recreated by Spiel is, in part, the story of two married, but unequal artists, and thus of a marriage in which the woman could very well find herself working to further her husband's career, while the latter followed professional callings and opportunities, as for example when Spiel recalls translating Mendelsohn's novel *The Hours and the Centuries* into German for a Swiss publisher (205).

Hilde Spiel's career as a writer was further complicated by her and Mendelssohn's decision to start a family during the chaotic and perilous time of the *Blitz*: that is by her life and new identity as a mother. As Spiel observed, it was a time when children were "conceived under bombs and born under bombs."[3] The story of her exile in England reflects problems and crises concerning the identity of a wife and mother in her relation to her family, her children, her husband, as well as to her personal and professional identity as a writer, and the resulting conflicts, tensions, and self-recriminations that such dual and often contradictory roles evoke. Spiel presents herself as torn between her role as a mother and her calling as a writer and journalist. Recalling her first journey in 1945 to Vienna as a war correspondent for the *New Statesman*, she writes: "...a bad conscience torments me because I have left Peter...alone with the children."[4] Still, Spiel presents the picture of herself as a woman who luxuriated in her presence at the cultural reawakening of Vienna, who reveled in concerts and private parties and gatherings. Nonetheless, her ruminations and reflections on having left her children for the first time culminate in the emotive words of her first daughter: "Dear Mummy, when are you going to come back from Vienna? I would so like to know" (233). Remembering her return from Vienna, she reflects both on her happiness at once again being with her children and at the same time the urge to depart on a new assignment: "Seeing the children again made me happy, but I couldn't come to rest. I wanted to immediately leave again."[5]

In recreating her second journey to the continent after the war, Spiel speaks of her "unsympathetic singleness of purpose," and her "heartlessness" toward her daughter and son. ("unsympathischen Zielstrebigkeit...Herzlosigkeit," 242) At another point she writes: "I have left the children for almost two months."[6] Such memories suggest confessions of a woman's sense of guilt at being unable to fulfill the emotional needs of her children. Spiel's most vividly remembered and portrayed feelings of anguish and guilt refer to the death of

her second child in 1943, who is remembered as the innocent
victim of human insufficiency, the victim of the negligence
and inadequacies of physicians and nurses. The girl suffo-
cated during birth: "I had wanted to name her, Brigid. The
following days were the worst in my life."[7] In remembering
and recreating those somber moments and days, Spiel presents
herself as alone and uncomforted in her grief. She would now
begin to discover the weaknesses and self-indulgent proclivi-
ties of her husband: "Peter wanted to be consoled by me...I
felt that I had failed at a decisive moment."[8] The memory of
the death of her own child leads Spiel to reflections on the
death and conflagration about her, notably the death of forty
children in a nearby school, innocent victims of the bombs of
the Luftwaffe, of man's inhumanity to man (Ibid). Spiel's
memories of the year 1943 are the memories of a year of
death, not only of her second daughter and the children about
her, but of the death of her destitute and psychologically broken father, the scientist, Hugo Spiel, who had also emigrated
to London (205).

Spiel's recollections of her life in London center equally on
Peter De Mendelssohn, who is portrayed in a highly critical
and pejorative fashion. That criticism, implied and direct, is
linked to many aspects of their relationship, particularly to his
continual absences that often coincided with crucial and tragic
moments in Spiel's life (204). In relating her father's death
Spiel reflects upon and criticizes the inadequacies of her husband, who emerges as frivolous, philandering and irresponsi-
ble: "Peter was not there to help, to comfort — it was as if he
did not exist — he only found out weeks later about the
death....Peter returned (from Germany) on the second of
August puffed up from successes and adventures of every
kind."[9] From the very beginning of Spiel's recreation of their
life in London, she refers to persistent financial woes (151),
and Mendelssohn's cavalier and totally inadequate attention to
finances: "Peter in his usual nonchalance did not set enough
money aside for us."[10] And she continues: "I had to borrow
money to have my father cremated."[11] Spiel's recreation of
her life with Mendelssohn during their London exile reads

occasionally as a justification for their later separation, indeed, as an apology for the dissolution of a marriage.

Mendelssohn is presented by Spiel not only as an artist with greater linguistic talent than her own, but as a personage whose views and allegiances were constantly changing, a figure laconically characterized at one point by Spiel as Peter, "the fickle one."[12] The characterization itself is provoked by Spiel's reflections and memories of her husband's putative criticisms and sudden rejection of British politics and conduct in postwar Berlin which entailed a criticism and rejection of the very people he had previously so much admired and identified with, and of whose country he had become a citizen. Fascinated by the Russians and enamored by the Americans (210-214), Peter became in Berlin, according to Spiel, a detractor of the British. He had experienced one of his great postwar successes in Berlin in 1945 by establishing *Der Tagesspiegel*, the first independent newspaper to be founded in Berlin in the postwar era. Having related Mendelssohn's successes and his new attitude toward the British, Spiel juxtaposes her own situation at that time with that of her husband: "In the meantime, I fight in England not only with grief and money worries, but also with a growing inner unrest, because life threatens to run away from me."[13] Spiel's pejorative rendering of Mendelssohn culminates in the memory of his insensitivities and alleged infidelity, notably in the recollection of his report from Berlin that he had just fallen in love with a "delightfully silly" "petite", (and) "very pretty girl" (238). Spiel confesses: "I cried out of anger."[14] While such revelations may be interpreted differently by various readers, they highlight and underscore Spiel's account of her unhappiness and misery at the time, her putative sufferings and self-representation as an abandoned woman.

Spiel's memories of the years 1936-1946 deal with the question and issue of identity on yet another level, namely with national identity. Recalling the celebrations in London following the capitulation of Germany in 1945, she describes her memory of intense feelings of identity with England: "Never again such certainty, to be at home here and no place else."[15]

Similar statements of Spiel's identification with England and the British run like leitmotifs through her recreation of her exile in London and the years 1945-1946, when she travelled on the Continent as a war correspondent in English uniform and under the protection of the British army. These emotional bonds with England were, according to her accounts, equally shared at different moments by her husband. Recalling the words of Peter in February of 1946, she writes: "I believe I could not be half as happy and half as satisfied anywhere else. England fits me like a glove....Let's stick it out for a couple of years. We will do well here."[16] Thus, the story of Spiel's and her husband's years in England is also a story of acculturation and adaptation, of their immersion in contemporary British literature and English journals, of learning to write and to publish in English, of gaining admittance to literary circles (154-157). Spiel's own quest for acceptance in the literary circles of London was, according to her accounts, difficult and problematical, entailing set-backs and numerous disappointments (Cf. 220, 226).

Following the end of the war the English writer Kingsley Martin observed that Spiel's and Mendelsohn's urge to return to Germany and Austria would be self-evident: "We knew it, but didn't confess it; nine years of adaptation in the English world had been in vain."[17] To remember the probability of eventually leaving England, was to recall the question of identity; and thus Spiel asked herself one of the most difficult questions that faced the exile after the collapse of the Nazi regime: "But where did we belong? Who were we? What had we become?"[18] The feelings of identification with England were, in Spiel's memories, deepened during the immediate postwar years, when she and Mendelssohn traveled and worked for the British or under British protection for three years: "...the unexpected and surprising happened: never before or afterward were we so close to the British as in the next three years, never did we feel so accepted by them as on the Continent, in the protection of their army."[19]

Remembering her reservations about leaving London meant to Spiel remembering a world and friends which she had acquired and cultivated over the years: "Should all of this have been in vain...the closeness to London's intellectual life, the close friendships, the close contacts with so many writers in and outside P.E.N., ... was my world, I did not have another."[20] As Spiel's *Die hellen und finsteren Zeiten* moves to final reflections on the disharmonies in her life, the inevitable separation from London and its consequences for hers and Mendelssohn's careers, the author shifts her focus to her memories of her first journeys to Vienna and Austria in 1945 and 1946. She reconstructs those journeys as confrontations of the present with the past, as a juxtaposition of the misery of the present, of the starving Viennese, with Spiel's identification and intimacy with pre-fascist Vienna. These are memories of the search for the very origins of her Viennese roots and for a lost time and place (226). Her journeys to Austria and Vienna are remembered as a time of being emotionally torn between her British and Austrian identities, a time of "großer Zerrissenheit" (231).

Even so these memories speak of her resolve at that time to never again become a Viennese: "I am sure that I don't want to become a Viennese for anything in the world."[21] That decision was predicated on what Spiel refers to as the virulent and persistent Fascist and anti-Semitic tendencies among the Viennese (236). And yet, her descriptions of her visits to Vienna continue to reflect the contradiction in her own feelings, for instance: when wearing a British uniform in a vanquished Austria. What she describes are feelings of "Schizophrenie" (244), feelings of a divided self. Her recollections of her journeys to Austria are also of feelings of longing and homesickness, "Heimweh" for the British Isles (Ibid).

Mendelssohn's and Spiel's decision in 1946 to work for the British occupational forces appears as a turning point in their lives: "The decision not to stick it out (in London), but rather to return to Germany was fateful—for after our three years in Europe the war generation of native Britons had in the meantime taken all the important positions—we were consumed by the German language, by the German world, whether we wanted it or not, and we could never completely find our way back into the British world, although we continued to write in

English for a long time and continued to vegetate in our London suburb (Wimbledon)."[22]

Spiel's willingness to remain in Europe for several years is
seen by her as symptomatic of her urge to break the bonds and
chains of domesticity, and thus her quest as a woman for self-
realization: "But I was also guilty. I wanted to break the
chains."[23] To have returned to England in 1946, would have
been, according to Spiel, to return to a life of boredom, and it
would have been in Spiel's words to prefer the life of feminine
domesticity over the much more exciting and rewarding life as
a journalist and free-lance writer (234-235). Again, Spiel's
presentation of her motives for not wanting to return to England in 1946 mirror the image of a woman driven by the urge
to break the chains of domesticity and conventionality. Her
quest for self-realization as a writer and journalist would
become the touchstone of her actions. Spiel's text conveys a
sense of the contradictions of life, of disharmony and loss on
different levels and in different contexts. While Spiel continued to work as a journalist for the British on the Continent,
she was at the same time drawn to the world of German jour-
nalism and literature, and to the German theatre. To leave
that world ever again and to find one's way back into the
world of English culture, politics and society seemed now
more and more improbable to her (255).

Die hellen und die finsteren Zeiten reflect's the memory of
Spiel's quest for self-realization as a feminine writer in the
perilous days of the Blitz, her sense of being overshadowed by
her husband, her gaining admittance to literary circles, and
being, however fleetingly and tenuously on the inside in these
circles. At the same time, the author also represents an image
of herself as an outsider, an outsider in both her native Austria
and in London, a figure who looks back on the accolades she
received during the war from such prominent British writers
as V.S. Pritchett, but who considered herself again to be an
outsider to the intellectual and literary world of London at the
time of writing *Die hellen und die finsteren Zeiten* (Cf. 219). The
sense of loss and disharmony emanating from Spiel's text links
it with many other texts of exiles. What makes her text doubly
poignant is her particular story as a woman attempting to

break with the narrow confines of traditional female roles, and reaching out for a new identity at a most unpropitious moment in history, when the bombs were falling.

10

Franz Jung's *Der Torpedokäfer*: The Perennial Outsider

In the texts of Spiel, Sender and Kortner their particular status as "the Other" stemmed from racism and anti-Semitism, and from the conventions of a male dominated society. Their texts reflect attempts to overcome oppression as Jews and/or women in anti-Semitic and patriarchal societies. An author can, of course, also elect of his own accord the role of an outsider. One of the most problematical, yet intriguing figures among the long list of outsiders in Germany in the first half of the 20th century was Franz Jung, who, unlike most of the exiles, left Germany only in 1936. Jung's autobiography, first entitled *Der Weg nach Unten* (1961), and later *Der Torpedokäfer* (1972) presents his perennial career as an outsider not only as the result of political and social forces, but equally as a consequence of his particular character and individuality. He writes: "I noticed very soon that I had gone out into life not to become a member of society, but to be excluded from society."[1] Franz Jung's reflections on his status as an outsider, on his continual exclusion from society, be it socialist or capitalist, in the East or in the West, plays a pivotal role in his self-representation as a figure condemned to isolation and suffering.[2] George Grosz, Jung's one time friend and associate from the circle of Dadaists in Berlin, characterized him as "one of the most intelligent individuals I have ever met, but also one of the most unhappy."[3] One thing remains certain: Jung was one of the most adventurous, radical, rebellious, colorful and problematic figures among left-wing German intellectuals before and after World War I. An anarchist, expressionist activist and leading figure among the Dadaists of the Berlin

circle,[4] he took part in the November revolution of 1918 in
Berlin and emerged as the co-founder of the German Communist Workers Party. He became an expert in economics
and a factory manager in the Soviet Union in the early twenties, a trade journalist in the Weimar Republic and later on
the editor of the anti-fascist journal *Der Gegner*, to name but a
few of his activities and callings. He was catapulted to notori-
ety in 1920 for his part in commandeering a German ship
which was subsequently sailed to the Soviet Union, a crime for
which German authorities would seek Jung's arrest for years
to come.

If we can speak of the autobiographical act as an act of self-
discovery, then it turns in Jung's case on his discovery that he
was destined by his childhood environment, by the social and
political chaos of the time, and by his individual character to
experience a life of setbacks, defeats and disillusionment, culminating in periods of withdrawal and resignation.[5] It has
been noted that the autobiographical act of reconstructing and
interpreting a life, is, in effect, an act of self-assertion in which
the autobiographer lends order, meaning and identity to the
course of his or her life. The exact opposite could be said of
Jung's text. Jung's autobiography reflects that the course of
his life, even before the Third Reich, was not one of continuity, but rather one of ruptures in identity, a life of discontinuity,[6] precipitated by a life of failures, a life remembered as
having been ruined, by Jung's time, by society, by others, but
equally by Jung himself. The development of Jung's life as it
emerges in his text, is not only the story of an individual's persistent exclusion from society, but of an individual's social and
psychological descent and fall, or as the first title given to
Jung's autobiography suggested, his life-story was, "the way
down" — "Der Weg nach Unten." Jung's descent, his journey to
the bottom, is presented by its author as a microcosm of modern society's descent into decadence and barbarism (479). The
failures in his life, as recreated by Jung, extend from his failed
career as a writer, as a husband, as an economics expert and
factory manager in the Soviet Union, to the failure of his
journal *Der Gegner*, which he had edited in the waning years of
the Weimar Republic. Jung's text is a work replete with

extensive reflections, including his ruminations on "biological determinism," a force, which, he claims, has often tragically affected the lives of men and women as it did, above all, his own existence.

The text begins with the reconstruction of Jung's gloomy and unhappy childhood in the East German city of Neisse. It ends in the highly negative reflections of the seventy-five year old: "I have overcome the ambition to be recognized as a writer, a businessman or lover, and even to be a decent individual, I am not decent."[7] Jung's text reverses many of the traditional strategies employed by autobiographers, foremost among them, the inclination to present oneself in the most positive light, hoping to gain thereby the sympathetic understanding of the reader. By way of contrast, Jung's often satirical and aggressive posture is designed, above all, to shock and repel his reader. This feature can be traced back to his beginnings as a Dadaist and anarchist, as well as to his cultural pessimism. Regarding one of his earlier texts Jung himself observed that his very direct and provocative style of writing often repelled the reader (67). He achieves the same effect in his autobiography with some highly pessimistic and aggressive reflections on life: "...We have already condemned ourselves. And you, honored readers, will not escape this fate."[8] Jung completed *Der Weg nach Unten* in 1961 during the Cold War, which was, however, also a time of prosperity in America and incipient prosperity in Germany, and, above all, a time of peace. After having lived through times of great political upheaval and having spent the last years of World War II in a concentration camp, Jung's reflections did not center on the need to secure and maintain peace. Quite to the contrary! "Down with peace!" he proclaimed. "And down with the delirium of a sick and parasitical society."[9] For Jung man is but a parasite in a decadent society and culture: "The society in which we are born ...is sick. It exhibits all the symptoms of an acute poisoning. It is sick because the individuals who make up this society are sick, poisoned, carriers of the infection."[10]

While many contemporaries of Jung, including the older generation of exiles, often lamented the tragic errors of their generation, they placed their hope for the future of Germany and the world in the youth of coming generations. Jung, on the contrary, asserts in his final reflections his opposition to and hate of youth. (478-479). The words hate and violence run through Jung's text from beginning to end. Thus, in recalling his earlier years of playing the piano and violin he concludes the memories of his foray into the world of music by saying: "I hate classical music.I hate all music."[11] Taken by itself and out of context, his alleged hate of music may strike his reader at first as amusing. However, it is, in fact, part of a pattern of expressions of hate permeating his autobiography. His hate of music is inextricably linked to Jung's perception of music as a means to control and suppress man's restlessness, his innate propensity to rebellion, and his anarchism (42). And this perception is tied in turn to Jung's memory of himself as a child abused by and alienated from the world about him. As for his friends or so-called friends, he states unequivocally: "I hate my friends. They are the ones who will refuse to follow me to hell."[12] Jung presents hardly any happy memories of his childhood and youth. His childhood hero — a brother of Jung's grandfather who had attempted to assassinate Wilhelm I — is remembered as an agent of violence and rebellion: "In the history of Prussia it was the first attempt to assassinate a Prussian King and Emperor. I was proud of it."[13] Jung's homage to violence extends beyond the violence perpetrated by individuals against society and its representatives, to the violence precipitated by nature. Thus, he relates how he luxuriated as a child in scenes of destruction and chaos caused each year by the flood waters of the Neisse, and conversely his disappointment when the rains stopped, the water receded and the chaos and destruction ended (29).

Jung situates the beginning of his life as a virtual outsider and his alienation from the world about him in his childhood and youth, specifically in the context of his problematic relationship to his parents: "I never understood my parents."[14] "...I only know that I was constantly shoved and pushed to the side."[15] In the account of this tormented and unhappy childhood the only person who is presented as truly caring for Jung, giving him support and a sense of belonging and protection, was, according to Jung, an oncle, who lived from time to time with Jung's parents (21-24). The story of this relationship is marked by nostalgia and by tragedy: the early death of Jung's protector in the same year as the death of his older sister: "The tragedy of this year struck me in the middle of the development of my character and personality. I was fourteen years old at that time."[16] The period following upon the death of his uncle and the death of his sister appears as a time of increased isolation, when Jung felt that he was less wanted and shoved aside more than ever, that he was in his parents' way and punished by them more frequently and without justification (27).

The memory of being pushed away, pushed to the side, recurs in connection with Jung's presentation of his brief stay at the home of another, decidedly less helpful and compassionate uncle near Leipzig: "My uncle immediately shoved me ...off to Leipzig."[17] Memories of perennial drunkenness, masochism and self-destructive behavior are central to Jung's recreation of his years as a university student, as are his memories of his search for openness and greater friendship among students, which allegedly made him leave Leipzig and study at Jena, a move, resulting, as Jung presents it, in further and deepening associations with failed students and drunkards: "I felt good in their company."[18] The story of Jung's life as a student reflects his affinity for and identification with society's outsiders and underdogs, with perennial alcoholics, users of drugs, and prostitutes; indeed, he relates his own thoughts of becoming a pimp: "I think at that time I was serious about becoming a pimp."[19] Drunkenness, indebtedness, masochism and violence emerge as terms with which Jung describes his career as a failed student (49). The resumption of his studies in Breslau ends likewise with his masochistic failure to take his final examinations, and his flight to Saint Petersberg to be with the dancer, Margot, who became Jung's first wife in a marriage, which, as Jung presents it, was destined to fail. His memories of his marriage to Margot are memories of physical and psychological violence, when the drunken Jung would be beaten by his wife (63). His desire to marry, he suggests, was in part the result of his fear of being alone, of being isolated

from others, a fear that would drive him into a marriage in
which he paradoxically felt even more completely alone and
isolated (61-62).   The pattern which emerges in Jungs self-
representation is that of his urge to be with others, with lovers
and friends, and of his inability to sustain such relationships.
The dissolution of his marriage is followed in turn by the
dissolution of later friendships, and the loss of such friends as
the psychoanalyst, Otto Gross and the poet, Richard Öhring.

   Jung's autobiography also looks back on his earlier autobiographical texts, foremost among them was "The Book of
Idiots" *Das Trottelbuch* (1911), a work linked to his problematical marriage. As Jung sees it, *Das Trottelbuch* was, in part, an
attempt to articulate his marital problems, and thus, a call for
help, which received, if any, only a negative reaction: "No
one came, no one talked to me. Never!"[20] Attributing part of
the failure of *Das Trottelbuch* to his provocative and unfinished
style of writing, Jung confesses; "As much as I know, the writer
is expected to perfect what he writes in order to draw the
reader or the listener into the text. I did not do that. On the
contrary, I repel the reader. There is no distance between the
reader and myself."[21]   The author presents his career as a
writer as one of false starts and failures. Moreover, it was a
career, to which he could only devote himself part of the time.
For he led for many years a double existence as a trade journalist and as a writer, always returning to writing in a life
which was perennially beset by financial problems and debts.
His vocation as a writer was further complicated by recurring
periods of self-ordained isolation (333), or by what he presents
as his inability to play a subordinate role with publishers or to
fight for recognition: "I was not willing to fight for my recognition as a writer. At least this is the way it seemed to publishers and people from the literary scene, who would have been
ready to help."[22] Jung structures his problematical career as a
writer and playwright in the period before World War I and
in the Twenties as episodes in a life marked by failure and
disillusionment.

   However, Jung's greatest disillusionment was his disillusionment in the Communist party, particularly during his
years in the Soviet Union. Communism and the nascent

Soviet Union had become for Jung, as he recreates them, surrogates for the missing family and home. They represented "the great experience of (his) life."[23] Recalling his arrival in Moscow in 1920 under an assignment from the KAPD, Jung writes: "That's what I had sought and what I had looked for since my childhood: home, the home of mankind."[24] And yet, Jung's experience with Soviet communism in the early Twenties was but the beginning of a new period of disillusionment and alienation, of a new chapter in his career as an outsider. The story of Jung's relationship to and work in the Soviet Union is the continuing story of alienation and isolation in a new context. He was soon dismissed from key positions in Soviet factories and enterprises. If in the story of his earlier failures and broken relationships he had used the image of the howling and crying dog shut out by merciless masters to characterize his loneliness and desperation (67), he now employs the image and experience of a novice boxer, to describe his own fate in the Soviet Union: "I felt like a beginning boxer, who is suddenly knocked down by a series of blows and is groggy....He gets up again, wondering where the blows came from."[25] Those blows, as described by Jung, would emanate from intrigues and party tactics. They signaled his gradual but inexorable exclusion from the building of a socialist society (255-256), and thus the beginning of his greatest disillusionment in life. He writes of his work in the Soviet Union: "In practical terms I was an outsider, a disturbing element...also a person with a messianic belief, who always remains a disturbing and destructive element in the building of a new society."[26]

The sequel of Jung's return to Germany in 1923 and his attempt to once again break into the literary scene continues the story of defeats and setbacks, which he attributes, in part, to his self-ordained isolation. The dialectical relationship between the individual and society becomes in Jung's text one, in which both the individual and society have entered a conspiracy aiming only at the exclusion, isolation and alienation of the individual Franz Jung. Indeed, one of the patterns running through Jung's text is the attributing of guilt to himself and others. When Jung does not remember ruining his own chances and fortunes by himself, then he does remember others doing it for him. Looking back at his last important literary enterprise, his failed editorship of the journal *Der Gegener*, he concludes that he was victim of the intrigues of his coworkers (387).

The purpose of *Der Gegner* was, according to Jung, to resist the decadence of the time and the corresponding rise of the National Socialists. One of the contributors to the journal was Franz Fuhrmann, who figures in Jung's biography as one of Jung's most important mentors.[27] His writings decidedly influenced Jung's perception of life,[28] particularly his belief in a biological determinism directing and shaping men's actions and lives. Jung's notion of the precepts of biological determinism underlie much of his perceptions of and reflections on the hopelessness of human existence, and, above all, on the particular situation of Franz Jung: "I suffer because I or the other individual is destined to suffer—he exists unprotected with a total lack of self-defense....The individual remains alone."[29] At this stage the metaphor of the dog shut outside howling in the cold night, or of the boxer who is continually knocked down, but somehow is able to once again resume the fight give way to the image of the "Torpedokäfer" (the torpedo beetle) which Jung observed during his captivity in Italy. As he describes it, the bug flies to its goal, a small opening in the wall, but then, failing to enter the opening, collides against the wall, and falls down. It recovers, resumes flight and the cycle repeats itself: "It is the biological quality of the torpedo beetle that it aims at its goal and falls....I have experienced the flight numerous times myself. The end was always the same. Collision, the fall, crawling on the floor and moving backwards to the starting point. Each time it required more strength....The wall against which the beetle flies is solidly built, generations stand behind it."[30] These images and metaphors are presented by Jung as moments of recognition, as a reflection of the self-knowledge he has attained through years of reflection, including the autobiographical recon-struction of his life. Society, be it capitalist or communist, will not surrender to an individual like Jung, whose character and social fate have destined him, nonetheless, to rebel and fight against it. The rebel

remains, if not destroyed by the eternal battle, always an outsider, always condemned to isolation, but equally because of
his biological code condemned to resume anew his life-strug-
gle, his battle against the impervious and indestructible wall
protecting society.

Yet Jung's anthropology, as presented in his text, does not
completely exclude the individual from participating in his
social destiny. The many self-incriminating passages in Jung's
autobiography, his confessions and self-accusations for his
willing participation in the demise of both his personal and
professional life, present the autobiographer as a self-flagel-
lant, and his text as one of self-flagellation. Moreover, Jung's
reflections on a biological code determining one's fate in society, namely the innate ability to adapt to society or con-versely
to collide with its values and morality can be read as an apology for Jung's own failings. Jung's development, as presented
in his autobiography, is the story of his journey into isolation,
his failure to integrate himself in and become a part of society.
It constitutes the antithesis of the ideal of individual development promulgated in the 18th and 19th centuries and articulated by such figures as Goethe in the context of his own life-
story. The rebel Jung asserted that it was of little significance
"whether the individual is accepted into society and nurtured
or excluded from society."[31] Such pessimistic pronouncements, which run through Jung's text, are inextricably linked
to Jung's perceptions of man's hope-lessness: his yearning but
ultimate exclusion from true salvation.

PART V

DEPARTURES, REALIGNMENTS AND EXPERIMENTS IN AUTOBIOGRAPHY

11

Robert Neumann's *Ein leichtes Leben. Bericht über mich und die Zeitgenossen*: Satirizing the Self and Rejecting Chronicity in the Autobiographical Act

The presentation of self as "the Outsider," and as "the Other" found in the narratives of such figures as Jung, Spiel, Sender and Kortner reflect, in the main, a gravity and seriousness corresponding to their memories of persecution, oppression and struggle. The humorous and comical, the interplay of human tragedy and comedy are with few exceptions stripped from their narratives. By way of contrast, Robert Neumann's *Ein leichtes Leben. Bericht über mich und die Zeitgenossen* (1963) features the exile autobiographer as a buffoon, as a target of his own satire, and as a 20th century Rip van Winkle. That the celebrated parodist and satirist, Neumann, would avail himself of parody and self-satire in the recreation of his life seems hardly surprising. Yet, another equally important mark of Neumann's work is a non-linear and discontinuous narrative through which he presents images and fragments of his life; and this discontinuity and rupture connects his self-representation with other characteristic texts of the exiles.

Franz Jung's autobiography reflected, even before exile, a life characterized by ruptures in identity. The exile's treatment of discontinuity and rupture extends from reflections on ruptures and breaks in their lives to the attempt to bridge those ruptures through the autobiographical act, and beyond that: to texts such as Neumann's, where discontinuity and

rupture have become part of the narrative strategy in the presentation of self. The following are but a few examples of the
ever-present sense of rupture, discontinuity and dis-harmony
in the exile's autobiographical writings.

The loss of citzenship, profession and wealth, of loved ones,
and of one's native language figure prominently in the exiles'
reflections. In the final lines of her autobiography, which
appeared in 1939, one year before the German invasion of
France and the beginning of a new period of rupture and discontinuity in the lives of the exiles in Third Republic, Sender
writes: "Hitler robbed me of my citizenship and property...I
was a woman without a country."[1] Alfred Döblin prefaced the
story of his flight through France with the somber and disquieting words: "How unjust, how shabby and pitiful to run away
from here....to have to flee...and flee again."[2] Hilde Domin
remembers how the exile was relentlessly pursued by Hitler
and his henchman: "For Dante it was enough to go from Flo-
rence to Pisa; he who was persecuted by Hitler was chased
through the continents."[3]

Stefan Zweig wrote: "...for truly I have been detached, as
rarely anyone has in the past, from the roots and from the
very earth which nurtures them."[4] Cut off, literally and physi-
cally from his past; without books, notes or letters from
friends, Zweig wrote *Die Welt von Gestern*, whose very title
reflects the sense of loss: "I have nothing more of my past
with me than what I have retained in my mind."[5] Zweig's
retrospective and Heinrich Mann's *Ein Zeitalter wird besichtigt*
converge in the authors' praise of the latter half of the 19th
century as a period of security, predictability and continuity,
which had not experienced the recurring catastrophes and
ruptures of the 20th century. Indeed, in almost every text of
the exiles reference is made to rupture and discontinuity,
whether in comparisons between the 19th and 20th centuries
or in citing examples from the exile's own life. Hans Marchwitza recalls his life as an exile in Europe as one of repeated
departures and breaks with the past, always accompanied by a
sense of loss: "Again it was time to say farewell. I thought of
the many departures, which I had already behind me in the
five years of emigration. After each something was destroyed,

each left behind a disappointment."[6] Linking his disillusionment with the separation from his family in 1938, Egon Schwarz observed: "...(it) contributed a great deal to my disillusionment, to the feeling of dissolution, indeed, to be living through the destruction of a way of life."[7]

For the exile cut off from his or her past, friends and acquaintances suffering the same fate and dislocation became coveted links to the past. "In emigration," Elisabeth Castonier wrote, "every friend, every acquaintance turns into a precious possession, a piece of the past."[8] The resurrection of a lost past and the bridging of the rupture of time is the purpose of Herta Pauli's *Der Riß der Zeit geht durch mein Herz,* whose title speaks poignantly of the emotional and heart rending trauma precipitated by the problematics of discontinuity: "This book relating my experiences (in exile) is supposed to build a bridge, connecting today with yesterday....A bridge beyond the rupture of time."[9] Many of the tragic suicides of the exiles, including Stefan Zweig's were, due in part, to the psychologically corrosive nature of rupture and discontinuity, leading to the loss of the exile's faith in his or her future, or even in the future of civilization. It was this loss, which led, according to L. Marcuse, to the suicides of Ernst Toller and Joseph Roth: "...both perished of a disease: the lack of a future."[10] Peter Weiss, a member of the younger generation of exiles, presents the ruptures and discontinuities in his life within the context of self-scrutiny and self-deprecation, as dubious justification for his failure to bring his work as an artist to fruition and for his inability to nurture and maintain personal relationships. The protagonist of his autobiographical novel *Fluchtpunkt* confesses: "Everything I did during exile had to take place under the specter of continuing and imminent rupture. This form of life had served me as an excuse for (my work) that was uncompleted, for everything that had failed in my work, as well as in human relationships."[11] As Weiss demonstrates, the memory and presentation of discontinuity can take many different functions in self-representation. The repeated experience of rupture leads, of course, to a sense of life's experiences, be they personal and intimate or professional, as discontinuous. The translation of such perceptions into autobiography is illustrated by Neumann's *Ein leichtes Leben,* in which a discontinuous narrative has become an integral part of the structuring of a life-story.

His book suggests that it was written in opposition to certain 19th century aesthetic preconceptions and assumptions articulated, for example, by such a figure as Wilhelm Dilthey, whose pronouncements on autobiography have continually been cited in theoretical discussions of the genre.[12]   It was Dilthey who asserted that life and life's experiences could best be understood by studying autobiography. The *sine qua non* of such a study was the autobiographer's reconstruction of the continuity and inner-connectedness (*Zusammenhang*) of his/ her life-story. *Zusammenhang* became the cornerstone in Dilthey's theoretical reflections on the genre (200-201). For him the classical forms of autobiography, illustrated by such works as Goethe's *Dichtung und Wahrheit* were writings in which self-representation mirrored a life as continuity. In contrast to this conception, Neumann's text reflects a 20th century sensibility,[13] particularly known to the exiles, namely the perception and experience of one's life as non-linear, as a life of ruptures and discontinuities, above all, as a life of disconnectedness. Neumann's rendering of his life-story reveals, as he suggests it will, holes and gaps, discontinuities and disconnectedness (44).

Neumann's perception and literary representation of life — the very antithesis of Dilthey's ideal of autobiography — is grounded in experiences which undercut and refute the 19th century ideal of life as progression, as a continuous and linear process of development and maturation. Central to the education life imparted to Neumann is, in fact, a skepticism toward continuity and linearity. Reflecting on the non-linear and non-chronological presentation of his life-story, he notes: "Although it is an unproductive thought, I wonder if it would not have been better for this final and last attempt to record my life if I had not started with my ancestors — then my parents, then myself, a, b, c, d,? But I have a deep mistrust with regarding our position in time."[14] The presentation of Neumann's life-story, which undercuts the Diltheyian principle of *Zusammenhang,* communicates an experience of life as a discon-

tinuous series of ruptures, breaks and fragments. What Neumann can promise his reader is, as he himself, suggests in a
typically self-deprecating fashion, only bits, pieces and fragments from "a faded and withered life."[15] Although divided
into three parts, his life-story is basically constituted of frequently disjointed fragments. Characteristic are the following
remarks, occurring at the beginning or in the middle of some
chapters: "broken off....Where, when, how to begin?."[16] "It
just occurred to me without any connection."[17] "There is no
direct connection."[18] "Everything is mixed up, there are
problems of chronology."[19] "I don't know...how it was all connected."[20] The function of these remarks is not merely to
stress the perennial problem of memory faced by all autobiographers, but equally to allude to the breaks, ruptures and gaps
in Neumann's *bios*.

Neumann's title *Ein leichtes Leben* is itself a tour de force of
irony. The unfolding story of Neumann's life is the story of a
life scarred by exile, by the loss of relatives at the hands of the
Nazis, by the loss of a son in the war, by the loss of a mother,
by the dissolution of marriages, and relationships, by the loss
of time, in short: by heart wrenching experiences, which lead
the ironicist to the inexorable conclusion that his was not at all
an easy life: "No it was not at all easy."[21] To remember and
reconstruct the years of exile, is to remember, above all, lost
time, time that had literally been stolen from Neumann (50,
505). At such moments irony gives way to self-parody and self-
satire, particularly in Neumann's reconstruction of the end of
his exile in London and his remigration to Europe: "And
...there I stood as...Rip van Winkel, someone had stolen the
best...years of my life."[22]

However amusing and humorous such self-characterizations
may be, they can neither conceal nor veil Neumann's recurring sense of disillusionment and tragedy as he recreates the
story of his *bios* and those who played key roles in its development. The fragmentary and discontinuous nature of Neumann's text thwart the reader's perceptions and understanding of Neumann's *bios*, particularly if he expects a linear and
chronological form of autobiographical narrative. Neumann's
rhetorical question regarding the problem of truth in the

autobiographical act merits comment in this context: "But whose autobiography gives a picture of whom?"[23] Through its juxtaposition of fragmentary and unrelated texts, and its reversal of chronology, Neumann's self-portrait calls for a reader attuned to the solving of riddles and puzzles. It is only after almost three hundred pages that Neumann begins to tell the story of his childhood, spent, like Kortner's, in Vienna at the turn of the century. Neumann speaks of it in a self-deprecating, humoristic and satirical fashion. Remembering his boyhood is to him a study in self-irony (see 308). Whether recalling the memory of other boys urinating on his leg (294), or remembering his early self as braggartly and parsimonious (297), Neumann interweaves a humoristic and satirical portrait of his early years. Recalling a photo of himself as a child, Neumann writes: "A photograph from that time presents me as dear and tender, with an innocent and half-open mouth of a child. Long carefully brushed hair frames a serious, touching face."[24] His reconstruction of boyhood is truncated and abbreviated; it is a caricature of Neumann as a boy, and thus it tends to distort the contours and salient experiences of childhood. Nonetheless, one of the char-acteristic features in Neumann's rendering of his life-story does begin to emerge in his recollection of his early years, namely an account of purported erotic triumphs (318), which began, according to Neumann, when he was five years old and continued into his youth, his university years, and beyond. Describing a photograph of himself at age seventeen, he writes that there was "an idiotic smile on his lips."[25] The photo was taken in a summer, when together with his girlfriend, he spent long hot days among the reeds on the banks of the Danube—virtually in paradise—like Adam and Eve except for the swarms of mosquitoes. Comparing the young man in the photo with himself at the time of writing his autobiography, when he was sixty-five, Neumann observes: "except for the sparse traces of the idiotic smile, the man in the photograph has as much in common with the man who is writing this as the man on the moon."[26]

It is, however, precisely the "idiotic" smile, which, seen in the context of Neumann's portrayal of both his successful and

his unsuccessful forays into eroticism, acts to satirize and caricature the autobiographical self. Irony and self-satire are constants, the threads running through an otherwise discontinuous and fragmentary text, often acting to camouflage the
autobiographical self. So are the recurring accounts of "erotic
triumphs," culminating in marriages and affairs, ending often
with painful consequences for Neumann's partners.

The fragments of Neumann's life, reordered and restruc-
tured by the author present a mosaic or mosaics. Neumann
fashions an image of himself as being at once the victim and
an agent of rupture and discontinuity: "I have again and
again separated myself from others."[27] This statement occurs
in specific reference to Neumann's separation from his first
wife and the mother of his son. *Ein leichtes Leben* is, among
other things, the portrait and confession of Neumann, the
putative seducer, a Don Juan or Casanova, the perpetrator of
ruptures and discontinuity in his own life and in the lives of
others: "My life with A broke up ...because of Linda!"[28] "And
I have not said anything about B."[29] It is no coincidence that
the three divisions of Neumann's text bear the names of
Tatjana, Griselda and Amalie, pseudonyms of three of the
women in his life. The story of Neumann's life is the story of
external and internal rupture and discontinuity, of the effects
of political rupture and discontinuity on the individual, but
equally of breaks and estrangements, that is of the ruptures
and discontinuities in human relationships. As such, it constitutes an autobiographical text as a story of beginnings and
endings, wherein the autobiographer fashions an image of
himself as seducer and adulterer, and thus as an agent of discontinuity and unhappiness.

Neumann's reflections on the course of his life speak of a
figure consumed by the problematics of discontinuity, be it in
the context of his personal life or in the larger political context, or in the lives and work of fellow exiles. He criticizes
Franz Werfel's personal letters for their inner discontinuity
(64), and attacks the apostate of communism, Arthur Koestler,
for what he considers moral discontinuity (133). His perceptions of discontinuity and rupture are additionally heightened
by his Jewish sensibilities, by being the part of a people whose

history is the history of the persecuted, a race fleeing from country to country, experiencing continuous rupture and discontinuity. The fate of his family in that history plays a key role in Neumann's attempt to reconstruct his ancestry, a process complicated by the loss of family documents, confiscated by the Nazis during the most recent rupture in the lives of family members (189). Relying on oral history, and at the same time, keenly aware of its pitfalls, Neumann first attempts to reconstruct the history of the men in his father's family. It is, of course, a history of rupture, precipitated by religious and political persecution, beginning in Spain, continued in Portugal, and, later on, in Russia, and finally in Poland, arriving finally at Neumann's father, Samuel Neumann, who was born in 1859. While Neumann is partly successful in reconstructing the history of his father's side of the family, he fails to uncover the history of his mother's family, a failure leading him finally to question his own identity. The family line of mother to daughter involves not only discontinuous places of residence, but uncertainty as to who, in fact, fathered the children of the mothers in the long "line of mother to daughter over these centuries."[30]   Neumann speaks, above all, of the rape of Jewish women: "My great grandmother who in her happy life was raped three times and did not get pregnant once? She was the daughter of a mother who was raped in one year of war seven times. Whose daughter was she really? Whose son am I? Who were my cousins? Which Prussian Junker, which dark Arab, which Soviet commissioner? My blood, my desires, fear, passion—whose fear and whose blood?"[31] To contemplate and reflect on family history is to conjure up not only the memory of dislocations and eternal wanderings, but equally the doubts of one's very origins, arising from the perception of questionable fatherhood in a world marked by the arbitrary and violent rape of women. The unfolding story of Neumann's ancestry is a story of ruptures and discontinuity, also in terms of rape. It culminates in painful and perplexing questions of identity.

The man who perceives and is sensitized to a multi-layered world of discontinuity about him, as well as in his own feelings and allegiances is drawn ineluctably to symbols and signs of the ever-illusive phenomenon and experience of continuity and permanence. Neumann's text necessarily includes the chronicle of a house in Kent, in which he lived in England during his exile, called the plague house (*Pesthaus*) which had retained for centuries its function as an isolation hospital for those stricken with the plague and other communicable diseases. Marveling at the continuity of this house, Neumann writes: "The surprising thing is the tenacity with which the house returned for six centuries to this function."[32] Describing himself as a fleeting owner of the plague house in the course of its long life, Neumann becomes the chronicler of its history, a chronicle including the names and fates of past owners. This chronicle, though discontinuous and subject to numerous digressions, pays homage to the plague house, as a symbol of permanence in an earlier world, which stands in sharp contrast to the discontinuity and disconnectedness of life in the 20th century, to which Neumann's text gives poignant expression.

If we are to speak of the understanding of a life through its recreation in autobiography, then Neumann's was, similar to so many exiles, a tragic one. However humorous, Neumann's self-representation and his representation of others is, it was not as the ironical title of his text seems to claim, "an easy life," but rather a life fraught with tragedy. As noted above, Neumann's text lays no claims to truthfulness in self-representation: "It is alarming that in spite of all intentions to the contrary that one still describes onself with less severity than all others."[33] By way of contrast, Ludwig Marcuse is preoccupied with the question of truth in self-representation. The true portrait of the autobiographer demands, Marcuse argues, often in a self-ironic and self-satirical fashion, full disclosure, including the history of the autobiographer's body.

Ludwig Marcuse, *Auf dem Weg zu einer Autobiographie*: Or Truth, Autobiography and the Body

Self-satire and self-parody also mark Ludwig Marcuse's almost solipsistic preoccupation with the self in *Mein zwanzigtes Jahrhundert*, in particular his erotic exhibitionism, though, stopping short of becoming what many would consider porno-graphic,[1] must be seen in part as self-satire. Faulting himself for his lack of courage, his failure to present his "true" or "complete self," Marcuse writes: "I find the source of its (that is: of his own autobiography) essential error in its lack of courage."[2]   This courage, to which the author so ruefully refers, entails both the courage to recreate one's life-story as a series of private affairs and professional defeats, and the interweaving of the history of one's own body into the larger and more visible story of his external life.   In point of fact, Marcuse found himself unable to translate his rigorous theory of autobiographical truth into practice: "I did not dare to write the history of my body into my life-story."[3]   This confession of autobiographical insufficiency, however self-satirical, sheds light on the subtitle of his text: "On the Way to an Autobiography" (*Auf dem Weg zu einer Autobiographie*).

The creation of "true autobiography" is linked in Marcuse's reflections on the autobiographical act with the autobiogra-pher's presentation of his most private history, namely the his-tory of the autobiographer's body.   In fact, the reconstruction of the history of the *vitae corporis* is to Marcuse's the *sine qua non* of true autobiography: "A life is not adequately depicted if the nature and social history of the hair, ears, the legs and testicles, the smells and gestures belonging to the soul are not shown ...."[4] This radical theory of autobiographical truth can be seen, in part, as the rebellion of a 20th century writer against a persistent 19th century legacy, namely the repression of the sexual in literature.[5]

In his own *Nachruf auf Ludwig Marcuse* (1969), the author returns to recreating, revising, and further enlarging upon his life-story as presented in *Mein zwanzigstes Jahrhundert*. Underlying his self-representation in this *Nachruf* is, of course, the feigning of his death. The "I" of his first autobiographical text is now supplanted by the "he" of the obituary, suggesting a — deceptive — ironic detachment from the subject of the text. At the same time, the *Nachruf* provides Marcuse with the final opportunity of writing the history of his body, which, according to him, must be presented as three interrelated stories, namely as the history of his physical appearance ("die Geschichte seines Aussehens", 103), followed by the story of the years of his physical prowess as well as those of his illnesses, his ("Gesundheiten und Krankheiten", 102), and finally, as the secret "history of his body" ("Geheimgeschichte seines Leibes," 110). The latter, however, often eludes reconstruction, because Marcuse finds that he has but vague and repressed memories of the history of his body ("blasse Erinnerung an die Jahre seines Körpers", 104). He presents this faint and failing memory of the history of his body in the *Nachruf* within a context of the maligned history of the body in Western Civilization, reaching back to Plato: "The fact that the individual exists out of a soul plus a dungeon of flesh cannot only be traced back to the bedevilment of the body by the Christians: Plato saw in the body a prison of the soul..."[6] As presented by Marcuse, the history of the body is a history of repression and neglect.

Self-knowledge is understood in *Nachruf auf Ludwig Marcuse* as the knowledge of the forces shaping and directing one's actions, tied to the history of the body and its maladies: "If he knew the history of his body more intimately,"[7] this would help him to explain his own particular quirks and idiosyncrasies, his impatience and sudden bursts of anger. Though the history of his body could never be completely known and completely described, it would, theoretically, encompass almost every aspect of it, from the sexual awakening of puberty to chapters on the degenerative diseases.

The recreation and reinvention of the story of the body, its life and decline, should not only turn on sexual organs and aspects, but equally on less celebrated organs and their perplexing and painful maladies, such as the bladder, the colon, hemorrhoids and hernias. (102-103). From the outset of his autobiography Marcuse emphasizes both his own neglect and the general neglect in literature of the fate of the body ("die körperlichen Schicksale", 35). The life-story which includes the history of the body is, in Marcuse's view, necessarily a tragic story. For the autobiographer who shows and tells all must in so doing recreate the story of the wreckage of the body's organs, their decline, their atrophy, an often ignored, unnoticed, silent and irreversible crippling of the individual ("ein ignorierter Prozeß der unmerklichen Verkrüppelung"; *Mein zwanzigstes Jahrhundert*, 35). Both the autobiography and the *Nachruf* define an ideal autobiography according to which the autobiographer would move from an external to an internal presentation of the self, a process comparable to the movement from outer to inner circles. This is not a movement in order to penetrate the psychologically interiorized self, but rather the history of the bodily organs. Moreover, in Marcuse's hermeneutics, the innermost circle of the body remains impenetrable. Marcuse's text ends in a paradox or feigned paradox: the "true" rendering of the self in the autobiographical act necessitates the replay of the history of the body which is, in large part, inaccessible to the autobiographer for reasons both of repression and of general ignorance. Marcuse presents himself as a victim of a spurious tradition. Ultimately, the history of Marcuse's body could only be written as fiction.

13

Walther Mehring's *Die Verlorene Bibliothek. Autobiographie einer Kultur*: Refocusing the Subject of Autobiography

The narrative perspectives of exile autobiographers often shift from the autobiographical "I" to the "we" of "the exiles" or "the immigrants,"[1] reflecting a consciousness and identity. This shift entails a movement away from the story of an individual, and the intimate details of his or her life. To be sure, the exile's strategy may also be to present a life-story or part of a life-story under the veil of fiction as in Peter Weiss's autobiographical novel *Fluchtpunkt* or Leonhard Frank's *Links wo das Herz ist* (1952) to name but two examples. Frank's text presents his life, in the form of a third person narrative, as the story of a pacifist and left-wing German novelist in the politically chaotic period of the first half of the 20th century. Frank himself appears as a fictitious witness to the fictional story of Michael who is, in fact, Frank himself. The shifting from "I" to "we", the presentation of the self as a fictitious character, and the marginalizing of the story of the self (e.g.in Heinrich Mann's *Ein Zeitalter wird besichtigt*) constitute each in their own way breaks with conventional notions of autobiography, with their claims that autobiography should focus solely on the self and impart verifiable information about the historical subject.

It could further be said that the student of exile autobiography is witness to a movement from the story of the self presented in the third person, to the extreme marginalizing of the self, and, indeed, the apparent eclipsing of the self in the autobiographical act. The exiles were not the only 20th century authors who manipulated, adapted and fused forms of autobiographical and fictional discourse. Thus, to give an example, Gertrude Stein's *Everybody's Autobiography* (1934-35) and *The Autobiography of Alice B. Toklas* (1938) are works whose strategy was to bar the reader from intrusion into and familiarity with Stein's inner life and person. *The Autobiography of Alice B. Toklas* is a classic example of a modern fictitious autobiography. The life-story of Toklas as told by Gertrude Stein is "an alibi for the presentation of the self" (Lejeuene, 47).

While Gertrude Stein set out as a fictitious witness to write the autobiography of her secretary and intimate friend, the exile Walter Mehring embarked on a much more radical enterprise, namely the writing of the autobiography of a culture, and specifically of its literature, an enterprise which, however, could not be separated from the story of Mehring's own life. Throughout his exile Mehring envisioned writing the autobiography as the story of a library, to which he was intimately related (284). He had inherited it from his father, the writer and translator, Sigmar Mehring. It had been presumably lost when Mehring was forced to flee Vienna after the Nazi annexation of Austria in 1938 (14). Mehring recalls that the decision to write *Die verlorene Bibliothek: Autobiographie einer Kultur* (1952) came to him in exile on a New England farm. It required a reorientation and refocusing of memory — from remembering the moments and chapters in his own life to the stories of books contained in the lost library. The remoteness and isolation of the New England farm allowed him, Mehring felt, to remember step by step what he had read in the library (271).

The translation of Mehring's readings into the autobiography of a culture constitutes both an innovation in the genre of autobiography,[2] and a merging of autobiography with cultural and literary history. Moreover, Mehring's text represents a deepening of the analytical and essayistic autobiography exemplified by Heinrich Mann's *Ein Zeitalter wird besichtigt*, where the story of Mann's *bios* is often eclipsed by reflections and interpretations of historical figures and the genesis of Nazism. On the other hand, *Die verlorene Bibliothek* is, in its defense of "the individual and individualism" closely related to Marcuse's *Mein zwanzigstes Jahrhundert*. Mehring's text contains paeans to individualism, individuality and personality, and to Goethe as one of their most important representatives and advocates (230). His musings on the lamentable state of the individual and individualism in an era marked by fascism and Marxism supply, however indirectly, the rationale underlying his decision not to write the story of the individual, Walter Mehring, but rather the story of a diseased culture, which threatened the very existence of all individuals as well as the genre of autobiography, as their preferred form of self-representation and self-assertion.[3]

In *Die verlorene Bibliothek* Mehring proposes to unearth literary artifacts the fanatical, irrational and barbaric undercurrents of Western Culture, the myriad records of human bestiality and barbarism, of torture and sadism, of genocide and political oppression; and thus, the prefigurations and antecedents to the barbarity and fanaticism of Nazism, to which he and countless others had fallen victim. The hermeneutical thrust of autobiography, the attempt to understand the development of an individual now shifts to the understanding of the life of a culture documented in literature and philosophy. *Die verlorene Bibliothek* is, in effect, a "book about books,"[4] which in its positive side looks back to the emancipatory ideals reflected in European literature of the 18th and the 19th centuries. These were ideals to which Sigmar Mehring had presumably given absolute allegiance: "....I was not so much interested in individual books as in the unique historical, aesthetic, and philosophical configurations in my father's library. Together they formed his particular horoscope of the 19th century."[5] The recreation of that horoscope constitutes a critique of the naivete of Mehring's father and his contemporaries, a naivete born of the optimism of the 19th century. For the historical, aesthetic and philosophical configurations upon which the optimistic horoscope was based, also contained, however veiled, distorted or concealed, a second story and dire prediction.

To what ever degree the books in the library articulated and reflected the emancipatory ideals of the 18th and 19th centuries, they invariably contained, in Mehring's presentation, the seeds of irrationalism and future political catastrophes: "My father, who was a model pupil of critical reason, would never have suspected that the germs of 'spiritualistic' epidemics lurked among the volumes of his library."[6] Seen from a different perspective, Mehring's conjuring up of the *bios* of the library is a re-reading of the intellectual biography of his father and in large part of the young Mehring himself.

Sigmar Mehring is presented as a personage who imagined that he and his fellow men were masters of their own destiny and in harmony with the forward march of history. Mehring's father's belief in socialism and progress insulated him, according to Mehring, against society's underground powers of irrationalism and fanaticism (21). More revealing and potentially more disastrous, his father was, in keeping with his generation, unaware of the possible evil effects of books, unaware of the "most dangerous components of the soul — genius and madness."[7]

Die Verlorene Bibliothek can be read as a critique of the illusions and deceptions of a discourse articulated by the books of Mehring's library. In other words: Mehring reconstructs the story of his father's beliefs and convictions, as recorded and codified in literature and philosophy, and passed on to the young Mehring, as a bogus intellectual guarantee of protection against political catastrophes: "In my father's library I grew up all too well sheltered. I was coddled in the illusion that human catastrophes could be averted — just as could venereal disease by timely medical treatment — by cosmopolitanism in literature, by scientific control of all experiments dangerous to the common welfare, by a general strike on the part of the international brotherhood of workers."[8]

Die verlorene Bibliothek presents the story of Sigmar Mehring's optimism in the progressive forces of reason, science and socialism, his reverence for writers like Emile Zola, and the books which immortalized those ideals and personages; but it also tells the story of a diseased culture. The indices and symptoms of that disease could be discovered, according to Mehring, in the "poison cupboard" ("Giftschrank," 60) of the library, replete with the infectious ramblings of anti-Semites and satanists, with books representing "the diabolic lewdness practiced by witches and heretics and the succubine wiles of women... (books) which developed torture into an applied science."[9] The "poison cupboard" contained the story of texts documenting a human predilection for irrationalism, sadism and racism, for the pernicious and infectious diseases of the mind and imagination. Thus Mehring's own forays into the "poison cupboard" of his father's library are recollected by him as an initiation into the vices and diseases of the human imagination (60-61). Mehring's reinvention of the *bios* of a culture speaks of the passage of these diseases of the human imagination into literary form and their subsequent appropriation by the agents of political radicalism and fanaticism, above all, by the advocates of anti-Semitism. In the latter vein, Mehring's ruminations turn on the uses of literary texts in anti-Semitic propaganda, and in the programs of genocide in the 19th and 20th centuries (59-61), as well as the exploitation of the writings of earlier anti-Semites by such prophets of racial purity as Alfred Rosenberg (59).

Mehring's text is above all, the story of a disease whose symptoms in the 19th century Mehring situates, largely, in the onslaught against reason—the irrationalism and pandemonium of romanticism, mirrored in the life-stories and texts of such authors as E.T.A. Hoffmann. As virtuosos in the art of mesmerization, of drawing and pulling their audiences into the unfathomable depths and vortex of the imagination (46-50)), they foreshadowed the greater and much more lethal art of Hitler and Mussolini. The reemergence of the disease of irrationalism in the 20th century was "nothing but the eternal unrest of romanticism," the emergence of the "most profound reality of the self", of Bergson's, "elan vital"... "The disease hit Italy as fascismo, introduced by Gabriele d' Annunzio, and it spread epidemically through the activities of a socialist newspaperman, Benito Mussolini."[10] The 20th century outbreak of this cultural disease is remembered and presented as a repetition of man's innate susceptibility to the diseases of the mind and imagination (169), which often led to the empowerment of the monsters of history, the Mussolinis and Hitlers, who, while they might be defeated on the battlefields of history, survive in literary and historical artifacts as "the symbols with which reality overwhelms us."[11]

Mehring's account of a library and culture also contains the story of prophetic voices, the cries of Cassandras, the warnings of such writers as Heinrich Heine and Fyodor Dostoevsky, who peered into the future and perceived the coming of tyranny and destruction (183-186), though their warnings went unheeded, while a diseased culture, in a virtual state of dissolution, continued on its collision course, its downward spiral and rendezvous with death and destruction. The principal victim of history's descent into barbarism is, in Mehrings reflections, the individual. The dissolution of the 18th and 19th century concept and ideal of the individual, of individual rights, as well as the ideal of personality and individuality; in brief, the ideals and rights for which Mehring's father had stood: "He (even) gave reluctant approval to bomb-throwing terrorism...he thought such actions must be undertaken for the sake of the individual against the state."[12]

The portrait of Mehring's father as a defender of the individual includes the latter's endorsement of radical politics and technological improvements which would directly benefit the individual's right to self-determination (31). As for the story of European culture in 20th century, it is for Mehring, the story of communism and fascism, of the emergence of the collective and of mass movements and the subsequent threat to the ideal of the individual and individual freedoms: "A vanishing upper crust was hypnotized by the sight of the herd, by the cries of 'Forward!' and 'Down With!' and by the hordes dancing around the individual burning at the stake....And the icy materialists were seized with a burning desire for the immortal collective soul."[13]

The "individual burning at the stake" is an apt metaphor for Mehring's recreation of the frontal assault against the individual, to which the futurist and fascist Marinetti would contribute in calling for the annihilation of the individual and the extirpation of the ego from literature (132). Mehring's autobiography of a culture is the story of dehumanization and depersonalization, of the atomization of society and of man in an age of uniformity and lack of character ("...eindeutiger

Gesinnungslosigkeit" 263). In contrast to the importance attached by Goethe to "personality, " Mehring finds that his own age regards "personality" as a "capital crime" (230). The 20th century history of communism and fascism, of collectives and mass movements is synonymous in Mehring's reflections with the decline, if not the death of the individual. Communism and fascism, the insatiable foes of individual freedoms, reflect what Mehring regards as one of the most horrific aspects of the spirit of 20th century culture, which with equal vehemence "demolished hotels that hindered progress, tore off the roofs of private life, toppled the coffeehouses, trampled under forests, meadows and pastures, the sanctuaries of creative individualism....Above all, it hunted down books that dealt with the pleasures and sufferings of individuals."[14]

Mehrings reinvention of the dissolution in modern mass society of individuality has, of course, a special significance for the writing of autobiography. His reflections on the individual as a threatened and dying breed, points to the undercutting and undermining of the philosophical foundations of the genre of autobiography as an expression of individuality. At the same time, the concept of autobiography as recreation of childhood, of youth, a career and of later years is no longer acceptable to him. Conventional autobiography, as solely the unfolding story of self and individuality, could never begin to address the very problems which led to the fall, banishment, and persecution, if not the annihilation of the individualist, Walter Mehring. The autobiographical enterprise required for Mehring an in-depth analysis of books, the remembering and reinvention of the *bios* of a library and culture. As he puts it in one of many dialogues with his father: "In your times fates turned into books; in ours, books made our evil fates."[15]

Die Verlorene Bibliothek can be viewed from different angles and perspectives. Foremost among them is the question of its credibility as cultural and literary history, including, for example, discussions of such literary movements in Germany as dadaism and expressionism. The intellectual force of his work derives from its attempt to uncover in literature the germs and viruses of a disease of the imagination. Its aesthetic importance lies in the reorientation of the autobiographical act as the presentation of the life of a culture. To read of the ideals found in the books of Mehring's father's library is not only to encounter the ideals of Mehring's father but to gain insight into the origins of Mehring's own early intellectual biography. It is also to read of ideals first challenged decisively by the advent of World War I and finally overwhelmed by the victory of Nazism.

Conclusion

This book has focused on self-representation in the texts of the exiles, and on the forms and functions of the exiles' autobiographical writings. Alfred Döblin's *Schicksalsreise* and Gustav Regler's *Das Ohr des Malchus* can be read respectively within the context of conversionary autobiography and its secularization. In the most obvious sense these are texts recreating turning points in the history of the self. Regler, of course,is only one of several former Communists who recreate their political conversions and political apostasy in their autobiographies. Other exiles recreating such turning points in their life-stories include Klaus Mann. In the final and expanded German version of Klaus Mann's *Der Wendepunkt* the focus shifts,however, from the turning points in Mann's individual life-story to the vision and hope of a turning point in postwar history, leading to the peaceful coexistence between the Communist East and the Capitalist West.

The influence of Augustine, but equally of Rousseau is evident in the confessionary and conversionary autobiographical writings of the exiles. Döblin's *Schicksalsreise* both reflects and renews the Augustinian tradition. The reception of Rousseau is apparent in Regler's and Marcuse's vanity and exhibitionism, and particularly in Franz Jung's self-analysis and self-criticism — in his self-flagellation and in his urge to tell all. Goethe's reception as an autobiographer and philosopher is reflected in attempts to focus on the intersection of self and historical circumstance, and on molding of the self in its interplay with the historical forces of the age. This characteristic of Goethe's autobiography can equally be discerned in Heinrich Mann's *Ein Zeitalter wird besichtigt*. On the other hand, Mann's denial of his individuality and singularity suggest rather a reversal of these key features in Goethe's self-representation.

The exile autobiographers, though they have adapted earlier forms of self-representation, often broke with them as well. Neumann's discontinuous text, his satirical and humorous, albeit tragic story is a case in point. In his preference for a non-linear and discontinuous narrative, Neumann rejected a narrative style grounded in the philosophical assumptions of the 19th century, assumptions as epitomized in Dilthey's observations on autobiography and illustrated in such works as *Dichtung und Wahrheit*. The Rousseauian model in autobiography—the conviction that all must be told is taken to a new extreme in Marcuse's musings on and delineations of "true" autobiography. Marcuse's rejection of public aspects in autobiography and his fixation on the private sphere culminate in his theory of an autobiography of the body. This, the most private of stories, which Marcuse postulates and demands of the autobiographer, is one that he himself paradoxically can never tell. Even so, Marcuse's explorations into an autobiography of the body, especially in his *Nachruf auf Ludwig Marcuse*, constitute a tour de force of satire, directed at Marcuse himself, as well as at the tradition of exhibitionism in autobiography.

Walter Mehring's *Die verlorene Bibliothek. Autobiographie einer Kultur* constitutes the most innovative departure from traditional autobiographical narratives among the texts of the exiles. This book about books, attempts to lay bare the diseased *bios* of a culture. From the beginnings of its modern history autobiography has turned on the story of self and individuality. The exaltation of individuality and self in Ludwig Marcuse's *Mein zwanzigtes Jahrhundert* can be read as a defiant gesture against the vagaries of historiography, and the consignment of individual life-stories to oblivion. It is a text whose philosophical underpinnings owe a great deal, as Marcuse readily concedes, to the radicalism of the solipsist Max Stirner and the militant individualism of Friedrich Nietzsche. By way of contrast, Heinrich Mann's *Ein Zeitalter wird besichtigt* cast the autobiographer in the role of a painter of biographical portraits of the great men of the age, including Bismarck, Churchill, Roosevelt and Stalin, and in the role of a historian interpreting the story of German fascism. These functions tend to eclipse in Mann's account the story of self and individuality. In many respects, Heinrich Mann elevates autobiography to a philosophy of history, reflecting the influence of such philosophers as Hegel.[1]

The exiles' fixation on history was inextricably linked to the fate of the exiles as victims of history, prompting the autobiographers often to present the period of exile as a collective experience. This experience included in its early years the specter of collective annihilation on the European continent and in England: "We felt like animals cowering before the lifted ax of the executioner."[2] Marcuse's words refer specifically to the precarious fate of the exiles in France, waiting anxiously for Hitler's next move. Echoing Marcuse's sense of impending annihilation, Elisabeth Castonier writes of her first years of exile in England: "We, who had fled from this man, feared for our lives."[3] Memories of fear and desperation on the one hand, and on the other, of hope in the ultimate victory of humanity over barbarism are interwoven into the story of a shared fate and identity. With the first allied declarations of war against Nazi Germany in 1939 the exiles could rejoice that the appeasement of Hitler was over: "We... rejoiced that the time of senseless yielding to barbarism had past."[4] Such reflections break the continuity of the story of self, shifting the narrative focus from "I" to "we," and differentiates the enterprise of the exiles from the earlier autobiographies of the Weimar Republic, as well as from autobiographies in the postwar period. The use of the pronoun "we", however, may also be presented in the context of the sense of guilt intellectuals and writers felt who believed they had failed to combat Hitler and Nazism.

At the same time, the exile autobiographer presents his or herself as witness to and an accuser of the agents and supporters of fascism and Nazism. *J'accuse* runs through the texts of the exiles like a leitmotif, and the targets of the exiles' accusations go beyond individuals. The recreation of the years and places of exile could be presented as a moral indictment of a host country, as is the case in the texts of Lion Feuchtwanger and Hans Marchwitza. In indicting France and America both Feuchtwanger and Marchwitza would avail themselves of the autobiographical report, *Erlebnisbericht*. This report on one's own experiences was one of the preferred forms of the exile autobiographer, particularly in the years of the Third Reich, when the exiles sought to mobilize sentiments outside the Reich against the Nazis. It was used by the early as well as the later escapees and survivors of Germany's infamous camps to indict and accuse their tormentors, and to enlighten the outside world concerning the barbarity of the Nazis.[5] Book I of Döblin's *Schicksalsreise* was also written in the form of an *Erlebnisbericht*, allowing Döblin to focus on and give expression in a direct and emotive fashion to his experience of religious awakening. As for the shorter and often truncated autobiographies of the exiles appearing in the first few years after exile, such as Toni Sender's *Autobiographie einer deutschen Rebellin*, and Martin Gumpert's *Hölle im Paradies*, they often presented the life-story of the exile up to the exile's flight or arrival in their guest country, reflecting the rupture and discontinuity in their lives.

In many instances the autobiographical texts of the exiles attempt to answer the question: How did exile affect the course of my life or my perception of life? The answer is as varied and divers as the exiles themselves and contingent on individual experiences, or more precisely, on selected memories of exile, dictated and shaped by the vagaries of emotions and personal agendas, or by politics. The answers range from Döblin's characterization of exile as his "salvation" (368), to Marchwitza's memories of American exile as a form of "hell," but equally as a test, strengthening the resolve of the Communist to continue the struggle against the demon, capitalism. Hilde Spiel presents her exile in London as contributing to her crisis of identity. In so doing, she portrays herself as a woman torn between her identification with England and with Austria, and torn at the same time between her role as a mother and wife and her calling as a writer. Robert Neumann, who presents himself in the self-satirical mask of Rip van Winkel, laments that exile cost him the best years of his life (505). Behind the ironic title of Neumann's *Ein leichtes Leben* lies the tragic story of Neumann's life, especially his life in exile. Gustav Regler remembers his exile in Mexico as a time of personal tragedy and persecution by former comrades, but equally as the time of his discovery of mysticism, leading to a new turning point in his life, or more precisely, in his understanding of life. But the answer to the question how did exile affect the autobiographer's life may be found not so much in what an exile states about exile, but rather in the articulation of a philosophical position. Heinrich Mann's visions of utopia in *Ein Zeitalter wird besichtigt* are the visions of the ineluctable march of history to communism and eternal peace. Such visions were surely born, in part, of Mann's materially and spiritually impoverished situation in exile in Los Angeles. Once the literary representative of the Weimar Republic and later the spokesman of the exiles in France, he was forced to exist in Los Angeles unacknowledged by the world about him and often on the edge of destitution.

The dispersal of the exiles to the far corners of the earth constituted for the Jewish exile, with few exceptions, a rediscovery of anti-Semitism, which was often either fueled or rekindled by Nazi propaganda. The young exile Egon Schwarz soon learned in La Paz "that there was also anti-Semitism here...our belief that we had escaped the fascist monster was an illusion....Hitler's poison (that is to say) modern political anti-Semitism had also penetrated to here, and I felt deceived, when after our arrival I heard an anti-Semitic propaganda speech screeching toward me from a loudspeaker."[6] Inside or outside the Reich, and before or after the destruction of Nazi Germany the Jews remained for such figures as Fritz Kortner always the threatened and persecuted "Other." Fritz Kortner's *Aller Tage Abend* recalls not only the exacerbation and intensification of anti-Semitism in Austria and Weimar Germany, but the perennially threatened Jew. It presents, above all, Kortner's mature career as a struggle against anti-Semitism, which becomes the justification for his life in the theatre. Years before the presentation of Kortner in *Aller Tage Abend*, Toni Sender had presented herself as a Jewish woman who had been victimized by Nazi anti-Semitism. Yet, Sender was equally, if not more so, concerned with the problematics of "the Other" from a different perspective, that is from the vantage point of a woman. In the texts of such women exiles as

Toni Sender and Hilde Spiel the definition of "the Other" shifts from the perennially threatened Jew to the perennially oppressed and struggling woman.

The autobiographical texts of feminine exiles are as varied and complex as the life-stories and sensibilities of their authors. Still, there are salient points which link their texts or distance them from each other. The problem of gender, and gender specific-roles and attitudes is central to the texts of Sender and Spiel. Spiel's self-representation is that of a woman struggling against gender specific roles, a struggle precipitating in her text her crises of identity as a writer, mother and wife. Sender's self-portrait includes attributes which belong to a decidedly male repertoire of self-representation. Still, Sender presents herself not only as a "man", but as more than a man, and as more than what she disparages as the "stronger sex". Martha Feuchtwanger's *Nur eine Frau* (1983) would seem to have been written by a woman with a very different purpose in mind: the casting of herself in the "insignificant role" of the woman, and conversely the idealization of the "most significant man" in her life, Lion Feuchtwanger. *Nur eine Frau* often reads as a biography of Lion Feuchtwanger. It is a text in which the author even luxuriates in the memory of preserving Lion Feuchtwanger's skin, which, according to Marta, she had peeled from his sunburnt torso in Italy: "I dried it and kept it in an envelope with the inscription: Lion's skin."[7] The list of exiled women whose texts speak not of self-assertion, rebellion and self-realization, but of the memories of "the great men" whose lives they shared, could of course, be easily continued to include such texts as Frederike Maria Zweig's *Stefan Zweig, wie ich ihn erlebte*.[8] The autobiographical writings of the exiles also speak of the breakup of marriages as is the case in Robert Neumann's *Ein leichtes Leben,* or violence between the sexes, as reflected by the memories of Franz Jung. Unhappy marriages are presented by Jung as episodes in the story of a perennial outsider, an outsider whose social fall was linked as much to his individual character as it was to the social and political chaos about him.

The texts of the exiles reveal affinities and divergences on different levels. Gustav Regler presents his story of political commitment and of self-sacrifice for a just world, as a life of heroism. It is comparable, in part, to Toni Sender's self-definition as a heroine and martyr. Yet Sender's text must be read with the autobiographer's intended audience in mind. The image she projects corresponds largely to the ideal of the "rugged individualist," particularly appealing to American readers, and the mythology of the American self. Moreover, Sender emphasizes that she was an unequivocal foe of communism, omitting any mention of one of her revolutionary speeches, delivered in 1919 at the Women's Conference in Leipzig, when she embraced and propagated the "dictatorship of the proletariat."9

The memory of this long and forceful speech delineating her revolutionary political and social agendas was excluded from her autobiography in an America still reeling from the Great Depression, and still in fear of the drumbeat of Communist revolution. However, Sender's book can be read in the context of the exiles' resistance against Nazism, and as an attempt to enlighten its reader about the nature of Nazi politics and terror. Lion Feuchtwanger's *Unholdes Frankreich*, while morally indicting French officials for their purported complicity and duplicity in the collapse of France, attempts to convince its American readers that the Germans were, in fact, not an invincible foe. For the French, according to Feuchtwanger, had allowed themselves to be defeated.

Politics and political enlightenment play an important role in exile autobiography from its beginnings to the collapse of the Third Reich and beyond, into the period of the Cold War. Ernst Toller argues that *Eine Jugend in Deutschland* explains the genesis of the Nazi victory of 1933. Political didacticism is equally a mark of Heinrich Mann's *Ein Zeitalter wird besichtigt* — in Mann's attempt to uncover the roots of German fanaticism and barbarism. Klaus Mann's *Der Wendepunkt* pleaded for new alliances between East and West, and for thinking in global terms, in order to prevent a nuclear holocaust. The deepening of his fears concerning the polarization of the East and West contributed to his suicide in 1949. Many of the autobiographical texts of the renegades, including Regler's, were written at different points in the Cold War for audiences in the

West, and particularly in West Germany. *Das Ohr des Malchus* was first published in 1958 in West Germany at the height of the Cold War in the Adenauer era in which Germany became ever more closely aligned with American strategies and policies for the containment of Soviet communism and expansionism. Regler's condemnation of Soviet Communism, however sincere, must also be read in light of the political realities of West Germany and the political fears and phobias of its citizens, particularly of its upper middle class citizens and the political Right. Conversely, Hans Marchwitza's vilification of America was designed for an audience on the other side of the Iron Curtain. The texts of both Marchwitza and Regler reflect an infusion of Cold War propaganda into the genre of autobiography, and thus a politicizing of autobiography, common to both the texts of Communists and renegades from communism.

While one may argue that the exiles, like most autobiographers, blend fiction and fact in the representation of self, the problem of truthfulness in autobiography takes on a special relevance in the texts of the renegades, as well as in such works as Marchwitza's *In Amerika*, which was written, in part, for propaganda purposes. As for the renegade, presenting himself in the best possible light to his Western audience, he may easily omit revelatory information from his autobiographical portrait, information which would tend to link his writing to Communist policies of repression. Moreover, autobiographical reflections on the problem of memory are a recurring feature in the texts of the exiles. Indeed, almost every possible comment on memory can be found in the autobiographical writings of the exiles, from the admission of a flawed and faulty memory, to the adamant defense of an autobiographer's memory.[10]

While many of the exiles' autobiographical texts reflect explicitly the political exigencies and politics of the time, this is certainly not true for all. Rupture and discontinuity in their lives and work could lead writers to perceive in memory and the conservation of memory an emotional and psychological refuge. In 1938 the poet Ernst Weiss asked: "What else is there for us to do in exile other than to live from our memories and to write our memoirs?"[11] To live from one's memories and merely to write one's memoirs was for exiles committed to the struggle against Nazism a defeatist and cowardly position. Yet for others it constituted, however escapist, an irresistible temptation. Stefan Zweig's *Die Welt von Gestern* (1944) is symp-tomatic of the use of autobiography as a means to escape the barbarity of the age;[12] its rhapsodic memories and image of Austria before World War I reflect an idealized, if not romanticized picture of Austria during Zweig's youth and formative years. The flight into the past permitted Zweig an escape into Austria's alleged golden age of security and individual freedom, a world which was, in fact, accessible only to a moneyed minority.

Autobiography as an escape, as self-justification for political apostasy and religious conversion, as an indictment, as historiography and biography, as the recreation of a struggle against anti-Semitism, as the celebration of self and individuality, as the story of "the Other," the story of victims and outsiders: all these varieties and many more figure prominently among the autobiographical literature of the exiles. Frequently, the exiles' writing of autobiography sprang from the urge to give meaning to a discontinuous and often absurd and meaningless period in their lives. On the other hand, the autobiographical impulse of the exiles also stemmed from the urge to communicate their experiences to each other, to build bridges over the ruptures of time and space. As Herta Pauli so poignantly wrote, the purpose of her own foray into autobiography was to build a bridge connecting today with yesterday: "a bridge across the rupture of time."

Notes

Introduction

1. Some of the other studies appearing in this period were Ingrid Aichinger, *Künstlerische Selbstdarstellung. Goethes Dicthung und Wahrheit und die Autobiographie der Folgezeit*; Petra Frerichs, *Bürgerliche Autobiographie und proletarische Selbstdarstellung* Ursula Münchow, *Frühe deutsche Arbeiterautobiographien*; Sylvia Schwab, "Autobiographik und Lebenserfahrung. Versuch einer Typologie deutschsprachiger autobiographischer Schriften zwischen 1965 und 1975,"; Wolfgang Emmerich, *Proletarische Lebensläufe*. Although Bern Neumann's *Identität und Rollenzwang* appeared two years before Olney's remarks on the dearth of critical studies on autobiography, it can equally be seen as a reflection of the renewed interest in the genre.

2. The best attempt to draw critical attention to the autobiographical writings of the exiles is found in *Exilforschung. Ein Internationales Jahrbuch* (1984): Vol. 2. This volume includes the critical assessment of several of the autobiographical texts of the exiles. See also the following: Wolfgang Müller Funk, "Das Exil ist eine Krankheit: Autobiographien als ein Mittel sich zu behaupten" *Merkur* 414 (1982): 1231-1236; Rainer Zimmer, "Zur Autobiographik des Exils 1933-1945" *Faschismuskritik und Deutschlandbild im Exilroman* 215-227; Mattias Wegner, *Exil und Literatur*, 151-169; Erna M. Moore, "Exil in Hollywood: Leben und Haltung deutscher Exilautoren nach ihren autobiographischen Berichten" *Deutsche Exilliteratur seit 1933*, 1-39; and my earlier studies "Crisis and Autobiography: Arthur Koestler's *Ein spanisches Testament*" *German and International Perspectives on the Spanish Civil War*, 45-60; "Einige Überlegungen zur Problematik der Exilautobiographik" *Exilforschung* (1984): 41-55; *Autobiographie als Geschichtsdeutung*" *Deutschsprachige Exilliteratur*, 228-241.

3. Herder first used the term "Selbstbiographie" or autobiography in print in connection with his theoretical reflections on the genre. See Herder's *Adrastea*, 229-230; also Georg Misch, *Geschichte der Autobiographie*, 5; further Günter Niggl, *Geschichte der deutschen Autobiographie im 18. Jahrhundert*, 38-39.

4. Southey is believed to have first used the term in England in 1809. Cf. John Pilling, *Autobiography and Imagination. Studies in Self-Scrutiny*.

5. Philippe Lejeune, *Le pacte autobiographique*, 13-45.

6. Cf. Frieden, *Autobiography. Self into Form*, 18-20.

7. In many of their autobiographies and autobiographical writings the exiles themselves reflect upon the arbitrariness and deceptive nature of memory, above all, on the difficulty of remembering. Cf. in this regard Lion Feuchtwanger, *Unholdes Frankreich*, 22; Arthur Koestler, *Ein spanisches Testament*, 193; Manès Sperber, *Die Wasserträger Gottes*, 119; Wolfgang Hildesheimer, *Zeiten in Cornwall*, 61.

8. Such exiles as Ludwig Marcuse and George Grosz readily concede the fictions and distortions of truth in their autobiographies. Cf. *Mein zwanzigtes Jahrhundert*, 387; *Ein kleines Ja und ein Großes Nein*, 7-8. Noteworthy in this context are also the comments of the renegade Communist, Julius Hay, on his flawed memory: "I would perfer to make smaller mistakes than exceed the limits of my ability to remember" ("Lieber sollen mir kleinere Fehler unterlaufen, als daß ich die Grenzen meines Erinnerungsvermögens überschreite" *Geboren 1900*, 14). Still, small and seemingly innocuous errors can under closer scrutiny reveal distortions of truth, often committed in a spurious attempt to present oneself to the non-Communist or anti-Communist reader in the most favorable and acceptable light. Cf. Hans Albert Walter, "Die Grenzen des Erinnerungsvermögens: Kritische Anmerkungen zur Autobiographie von Julius Hay", 107-116. Gustav Regler's self-representation in his autobiography *Das Ohr des Malchus* is an example of self-glorification par excellence. See chapter 2 of this study. Other exile writers and intellectuals emphasized that their memory was in no way faulty, or that their recreations of their lives contained only facts and the truth. Cf. Stefan Zweig, *Die Welt von Gestern*, 12; Marta Feuchtwanger, *Nur eine Frau*, 5; Kurt Hiller, *Eros*, 20. Such claims to truth in self-representation and in the presentation of others can be seen as a strategy to meet the expectations of the reader harboring the literalist or purist view of autobiography.

9. Paul John Eakin, *Fictions in Autobiography. Studies in the Art of Self-Invention*.

10. Johnathan Loesberg, *Fictions of Consciousness*.

11. Michael Sprinker, "Fictions of Self.The End of Autobiography."

12. Hans Robert Jauß, "Literaturgeschichte als Provokation der Literaturwissenschaft", 144-250.

13. See Klaus Detleff-Müller, "Die Autobiographie der Goethezeit", 479; Sandra Frieden, *Autobiography. Self into Form*, 29.

14. Instances where German writers have continued to follow the model of *Dichtung und Wahrheit* can be found in the autobiographies of Hans Carossa, Gerhardt Hauptmann, Friedrich Georg Jünger and Hermann Bahr. See Ingrid Aichinger, *Künstlerische Selbstdarstellung*, 33. Such features of *Dichtung und Wahrheit* as the interplay of self and historical cir-

cumstance are also reflected in Heinrich Mann's *Ein Zeitalter wird besichtigt*, but the emphasis on individuality is thoroughly rejected. See chapter 3.

15. "Die Selbstbiographie ist die höchste und am meisten instrucktive Form, in welcher uns das Verstehen des Lebens entgegentritt." Dilthey, *Gesammelte Schriften* VII, 199.

16. Cf. Helmut Pfanner, *Exile in New York*, 17; Egon Schwarz, "Was ist und wozu studiert man Exilliteratur?", 15.

17. "Wer den Zusammenbruch von 1933 in Deutschland begreifen will, muß die Ereignisse der Jahre 1918 und 1919 in Deutschland kennen...." Toller, *Eine Jugend in Deutschland*, 7.

18. "Wir sind gescheitert, alle. Alle begingen Fehler, alle trifft Schuld....Die Kommunisten ebenso wie die Unabhängigen" (Ibid, 112).

19. "Wir die Verräter unserer Selbst tragen in dem Gepäck unseres Exils, Goethe und Hölderlin, Novalis und Kleist. Wie haben wir, die Erben dieses Imperiums des Geistes verwaltet? Zuschanden ist die Idee der Freiheit, die dies alles erzeugte, ausgeliefert einer stupiden Gewalt, und ärger als Bettler stehen wir da mit unserer sinnlosen Habe." Gumpert, *Hölle im Paradies. Selbstdarstellung eines Arztes*, 278.

20. "Was tat ich selbst zur Besserung und zum Schutze unserer so sehr schutz-und besserungsbedürftigen Demokratie? Wo war mein eigener Beitrag zur Rettung der gefährdeten Republik? Welcher kämpferischen Tat oder sozialen Leistung konnte ich mich rühmen"? Mann, *Der Wendepunkt*, 250.

21. "Aber was, frage ich mich, habe ich selber eigentlich aufgeboten, um sie zu vernichten? Mit dem Ekel ist es nicht getan." Döblin, *Schicksalsreise*, 204.

22. "Wir haben versäumt, als unsere Zeit und unsere Stunde war, ihnen zuvorzukommen....Wir, die wir berufen gewesen wären, dem entgegenzuwirken, haben zu lange gezögert, uns mit dem profanen Odium der Tagespolitik zu belasten. Wir lebten zu sehr in der Splendid Isolation des Geistes und der Künste." Zuckmayer, *Als Wär's ein Stück von mir*, 381-382.

23. "Viele sogenannte Intellektuelle erklärten voll Stolz, daß sie sich nicht im geringsten für Politik interessierten und daher nichts davon wüßten." Sender, *Autobiographie einer deutschen Rebellin*, 177.

24. "Wie weit die nationalsozialistischen Wühlmäuse sich vorgestellt hatten, ahnte niemand in unserem kleinen Kreis, der sich amüsieren, tanzen und verlieben wollte." Castonier, *Stürmisch bis heiter. Memoiren einer Außenseiterin*, 144.

25. "Lange trug ich die Schuld, daß ich nicht zu denen gehörte, die die Nummer der Entwertung ins Fleisch eingebrannt bekommen hatten, daß ich entwichen und zum Zuschauer verurteilt worden war. Ich war aufgewachsen, um vernichtet zu werden, doch ich war der Vernichtung entgangen." Weiss, *Fluchtpunkt*, 212.

26. "Hier sei gesagt: Hugenberg und seine Partei sind für den Niedergang Deutschlands in die Barbarei verantwortlich. Sie gaben dem Aufstieg Hitlers den äußeren Anschein der Legalität. Hugenberg machte die Nazis gesellschaftsfähig." Sender, *Autobiographie einer deutschen Rebellin*, 241.

27. Cf. Heinrich Mann, *Ein Zeitalter wird besichtigt*, 293.

28. "...antihumanistischen, antichristlichen Radikalismus, den irrationalen Vehemenz der Hitler Bewegung." Mann, *Der Wendepunkt*, 248.

29. "Wie leicht wäre es für die Welt gewesen, alle diese bedrohten Menschen zu retten. Aber sie verschloß sich in Argwohn, Haß und Selbstsucht den Verfolgten Unterschlup...und trägt die Mitverantwortung für das grauenhafte Schicksal, das so viele ereilte." Schwarz, *Keine Zeit für Eichendorff*, 334.

30. "Ulbricht betrieb Verrat für sein eigenes Fortkommen ....Ulbricht denunzierte Rivalen in seiner Partei....Ulbricht spionierte." Regler, *Das Ohr des Malchus*, 231.

Chapter I Alfred Döblin, *Schicksalsreise*

1. "...kein bewegtes äußeres Leben...dessen Beschreibung abenteuerliche oder originelle Situationen aufzeigen könnte." Döblin, "Ich nähere mich den Vierzig", 13.

2. "Gibt es einen Vater, zu dem man aufblicken kann? So schön einlüllend müßte das sein. Es ist schlimm für jemand wie mich, daß er viele Stunden über, Tage, ja Monate gehetzt ist und niemand ihn aufnimmt. Ein Gott — es ist ein schöner Gedanke" (12).

3. "Darum schreibe ich dies auf. Denn es darf nicht sein, daß solche außerordentliche Geschehen nur wie ein Lichtschein über mich huscht...." Döblin, *Schicksalsreise*, 116.

4. "Einmal las ich, seit langer Zeit wieder einmal, die Bekenntnisse des heiligen Augustinus" (354).

5. "...ein einzigartiger Lernprozess" (Ibid).

6. "Damit endet nicht die Schicksalsreise, sondern was ich von ihr zu berichten habe" (147).

7. "Meine Worte bedeuteten hier nichts, und ich empfing nichts, wieder eine Fahne, die ich nicht halten konnte" (212).

8. "lauter Enttäuschte und Desillusionierte" (Ibid).

9. "Ich habe ja auch geschrieben. Half es mir. Sicherte es mich? Was war es?" (213).

10. "Ein stiller Vorgang hinter geschlossenen Türen" (213).

11. "In mir setzte sich 1932 ein merkwürdiges Bild fest....ein uralter, verschlimmerter Gott verläßt vor dem Eintritt der letzten Verwesung seinen himmlischen Wohnsitz; ein düsterer Strafbefehl, dem er sich nicht entziehen kann, zwingt ihn auf die Erde herunter. Er soll büßen für seine alten Sünden. Und so wandert er durch das heiße Land....Was war das? Es wurde mir erst beim Schreiben dieser baylonischen Wanderung klar: Es war das Gefühl meiner eigenen verlorenen Situation. Es war das Gefühl von Schuld, vieler Schuld, großer Schuld. Unerträglich war es geworden, und der Wille zum Entrinnen ließ nicht nach....Es war die Vorwegnahme des Exils, und noch vieles mehr" (367).

12. As Hans Graber has aptly written: "For Döblin Germany had already become unbearable before 1933, and not only politically, but also spiritually. Perhaps this can help to explain the otherwise inexplicable confidence which the emigrant expressed at the beginning of his exile in the form of a quote from Schiller: But it was his salvation; it lifted him up" ("Für Döblin war Deutschland schon vor 1933, nicht nur politisch, auch geistig unerträglich geworden. Vielleicht erklärt sich daraus die sonst durch nichts begründete Zuversicht, die der Emigrant am Anfang gern in Form eines Schiller-Zitats äußerte:'Doch es ward ihm zum Heil, es riß ihn nach oben." "Politisches Postulat und autobiographischer Bericht. Zu einigen im Exil entstandenen Werken Alfred Döblins," 419. Wulf Koepke's study on Döblin's flight through France does not focus on Döblin's religious awakening, but rather on Döblin's and other exiles'reactions to the fall of France. "Die Flucht durch Frankreich: Die zweite Erfahrung der Heimatlosigkeit in Berichten der Emigranten aus dem Jahr 1940" *Exilforschung* Vol.4; 229-242. For the most part, Döblin's report of his religious awakening and conversion was received critically, if not negatively by the press. See *Alfred Döblin im Spiegel der Kritik*, 417-424.

13. "Eine Niederlage war gekommen. Die Niederlage, eine große Niederlage, drang in mich ein. Ich ging ihr entgegen" (151).

14. "Er behielt mich im Auge...er ließ nicht los...er griff ein" (301).

15. "Die Welt ist Geschichte, Tat—und die Person ist herrlich daran beteiligt. Es gibt keinen Tod" (356).

16. "Man darf den geheimen Kräften nicht widersetzen, die unser Schicksal leiten" (222).

Chapter 2 Gustav Regler, *Das Ohr des Malchus*

1. See David Pike, *German Writers in Soviet Exile 1933-1945*, 98, 357.

2. Cf. Arthur Koestler, *The Invisible Writing*, Julius Hay, *Geboren 1900*, Manès Sperber, *Die vergebliche Warnung* and *Wie eine Träne im Ozean*, Alfred Kantorowicz, *Deutsches Tagebuch*. For a detailed account of Regler's break with the party see Ralph Schock, *Gustav Regler-Literatur und Politik 1933-1940*, 471-481.

3. "Wer überhaupt das Recht zum Gericht hat?" Regler, *Das Ohr des Malchus*, 507.

4. "Ich fürchte Diktatoren nicht" (239).

5. Regler states of his motives for supporting the Bavarian revolution: "I wanted to make Munich into a garden of Eden." ("Ich wollte München zum Garten Eden machen" (108).

6. "Ich habe nie einen Kampf begonnen, weil ich des Sieges sicher war" (300).

7. Regler's wrestling with the moral dilemma posed by the doctrine of political expediency—ends justifying the means—was, of course, not unique, but rather symptomatic of the plight of the political apostates, or so they would have their readers believe. Cf. particularly in this context Koestler's *The Gladiators* (1939) and *Darkness at Noon* (1941).

8. David Pike argues that Kamenev was already in prison awaiting his execution by the time Regler arrived in Moscow in 1936. Op. cit., 109.

9. In *Juanita-ein Roman aus dem spanischen Bürgerkrieg* Regler presented the power tactics and plays of communism as being as morally bankrupt as those of its fascist antagonist. See Hans-Dieter Petto, "Auf der Suche nach dem Jenseits der Politik. 'Juanita,' Gustav Reglers anderer Spanienkriegroman" *Gustav Regler. Dokumente und Analysen*, 223-234.

10. "Warum das Leben einer Frau vergällen?" Regler, *Das Ohr des Malchus*, 177.

11. "Mit welchem Recht hatte ich diese Frau in dieses von Problematik schwere Exilleben gezogen?" (215).

12. "Das Schuldgefühl diese Frau 1933 aus Deutschland weggelockt zu haben" (413).

13. "An diesem Tag, dessen bin ich sicher, begann ihre Krankheit. Sie schluckte das Gift des Abscheus hinein" (492).

14. "Ein Sieg der Farbe gegen die Nacht...der Zartheit gegen die Brutalität, der Harmonie gegen das Chaos der Zellen" (502).

15. "Erinnerungen abwerfen wie schmutzige Verbände" (483).

16. "Fängt es wirklich wieder von neuem an?" (507).

17. "Manifestation menschlicher Unzulänglichkeit" (445).

Excursus: History and Exile Autobiography

1. "Die Weltgeschichte brachte mich...um die intimere Bekanntschaft mit diesem ehrwürdigen Institut." Schwarz, *Keine Zeit für Eichendorff*, 46.

2. "Ich müßte diese Geschichte so fortsetzen, wie sie hätte weitergehen können, ja, wie sie hätte weitergehen müssen, wenn mein böser Weggefährte, das XX Jahrhundert, nicht alles durcheinandergebracht hätte." Hay, *Geboren 1900*, 119.

3. "...der Aufeinanderfolge von Katastrophen, deren Zeugen und Opfer unsere Generation seit 1914 gewesen ist." Zweig, *Die Welt von Gestern*, 289.

4. "...ein (en) groß (en) Tag in der Geschichte." Mann, *Der Wendepunkt*, 503.

5. "Nun geht es weiter, fragt sich nur in welcher Richtung es weiter geht. Wir können uns für die richtige entscheiden oder die falsche. Die falsche wird immer falscher, immer gefährlicher....Noch ein paar Schritte auf den Abgrund zu, und wir stürzen hinein, kopfüber. Der finale Wendepunkt wäre erreicht, das episodenreiche Drama abgeschlossen" (ibid).

6. "Jeder Schritt, der uns von diesem Ziel entfernt, tendiert zum Abgrund" (ibid).

7. "Von dem Ausgang der papierenen Schlacht um die Gehirne wird es abhängen, ob es zur Atomschlacht um die Kontinente kommen wird." Frei, *Der Papiersäbel*, 273-274.

Chapter 3 Henrich Mann, *Ein Zeitalter wird besichtigt*

1. Cf. *Die Zeit* 8 January 1982, 15.

2. See the preface to Goethe's *Dichtung und Wahrheit*.

3. "Es wird Zeit, daß ich mich vorstelle. Mein Name ist Jx." Mann, *Ein Zeitalter wird besichtigt*, 147.

4. "Meinesgleichen kommt überall vor....was ich denke, mache und kann, sollte eigentlich jeder fertigbringen" (ibid).

5. "Jx, die zahllosen Personen dieses Namens, haben für die...Sieger dieses Krieges...Stellung genommen" (150).

6. "Jx denkt, viele Jx...denken" (166).

7. "Dieselben Gespräche fanden längst statt, zwischen anderen Jx, die tot, aber um so namhafter sind" (167).

8. See Renate Werner, ed., *Heinrich Mann.Texte zu seiner Wirkungsgeschichte in Deutschland*, 129-187.

9. "Eine Autobiographie sieht am besten von ihrem Urheber ab....Er trete als Augenzeuge auf—der Ereignisse und seiner selbst" (147).

10. "Das Zeitalter, in das er verwickelt ist, interpretiert ihn...." (450).

11. "War ich ein Kämpfer? Ich gestaltete, was ich sah und suchte mein Wissen überzeugend, wenn es hoch kam, auch anwendbar zu machen" (223).

12. "Bei ihm allein finde ich unverzeihlich, daß er nichts ändern konnte" (150).

13. "Wer abreist und nichts zurückläßt als nur Unheil....sucht einige Tröstung, sogar Rechtfertigung, bei einer Anonymität..." (449).

14. Cf. Ingrid Aichinger, *Künstlerische Selbstdarstellung*, 184-192.

15. "Er hat, von 1875-1890, den Frieden nicht nur erhalten, ihn auch stark gemacht. Dank dem Fürsten ist der Friede...noch fünfundzwanzig Jahre fähig gewesen zu dauern, gegen Übermut und bösen Willen" (179).

16. "Damit eine ganze Jugend einheitlich sei, sich 'historisch entwickele,' mit einem Ausdruck des 19. Jahrhunderts, muß man glauben können, ihr Ablauf sei logisch begründet—was aufhört, wenn Krieg ist, Kriege sind der gewaltsame...Bruch in einem Leben, das sonst zusammenhing" (179).

17. Because of Heinrich Mann's effusive praise of communism and Stalin, he was unable to find a publisher for the book in the United States or in South America. See my article "Heinrich Mann's View of History and the Allied Leaders in *Ein Zeitalter wird besichtigt*" *Der zweite Weltkrieg und die Exilanten*, 221.

18. For a more detailed discussion of this aspect of Mann's image of the Allied Leaders see "Heinrich Mann's View of History and the Allied Leaders", 222-227.

19. "Dies wären unpersönliche Feststellungen? Es sind die allerpersönlichsten" (158).

20. "Mein... Dasein hängt ganz und gar davon ab, daß sittliche Bemühungen möglich sind" (158).

21. "Der Staatsmann Churchill hat seine Wurzel in dem Schriftsteller Churchill" (32).

22. "Ich kannte den König Henri Quatre von Frankreich: er hatte durchaus das gleiche im Sinn..., wie Messrs. Churchill und Roosevelt" (493).

23. "Ich erlebe nichts anders als die Völker; sie haben zweifellos gefühlt wie ich....Die Nachricht von dem Pakt—dem Verrat, der Katastrophe hatte mich erschüttert wie jeden" (139).

24. "Zusammenhänge gibt es, man entziffert sie wohl, unter der Bedingung, daß man schon dabei war und nachher lange genug gelebt" (11).

25. "Ich ... weiß, daß die Zusammenhänge weit zurückführen" (28).

26. Cf. David Caute, *The Fellow Travellers*, 251.

27. "Ein neuer Mensch, ein neues Zeitalter nehmen ihren Anfang hier" (509).

28. "Ich besichtige ein Zeitalter....Es hat mehr getaugt als ich" (504).

Chapter 4 Ludwig Marcuse, *Mein zwanzigstes Jahrhundert*

1. Harold von Hofe has stressed precisely the importance of Marcuse's text as a source book for the study of German literature in exile: "The book is indispensible for researchers as a source for the years of German literature in exile, in France and Los Angeles" ("Als Quelle für die Jahre der deutschen Literatur im Exil, in Frankreich und in Los Angeles, ist der Band für die Forschung unentbehrlich"). "Ludwig Marcuse" *Deutsche Exilliteratur seit 1933*, 539. He characterizes Marcuse's text as an "unsparing, uninhibited and courageous presentation" ("schonungslose, hemmungslose und mutige Darstellung", ibid). Yet, perhaps for the lack of space in his brief article, he is not able to go into sufficient detail concerning Marcuse's fixation on the self and individuality—on the quirks and singularity of Ludwig Marcuse, and his paean to the individual and individual freedoms and pleasures. Above all, he fails to take into account Marcuse's denigration of historiography and the historiographer's presentation of the great actors and movers of history.

2. "Ich schreibe hier nicht Literaturgeschichte, nicht einmal eine Geschichte der exilierten Literatoren." Marcuse, *Mein zwanzigstes Jahrhundert*, 282.

3. "Wenigstens in meinem Leben folgte das Bewußtsein nicht dem Sein" (65).

4. "...ich erzähle eine jener Lebensgeschichten, von denen Hegel sagte, sie ständen auf den leeren Seiten im großen Buch der Erinnerung. Mir scheinen im Gegensatz zu ihm, diese Millionen leeren Seiten denkwürdiger zu sein als die bedruckten" (38).

5. "Das Unbehagen des Einzelnen an seiner Singularität" (312).

6. "Der große Mann schreibt nicht eine Autobiographie, sondern Weltgeschichte, sofern er mit ihr identisch ist" (381).

7. "Ich glaubte immer..., daß trotz aller Weltgeschichte, im Einzelnen die Welt beginnt und endet" (239).

8. "Mir geht nichts über mich" (64).

9. "Ich liebte jetzt G.B. mehr als je....Scheidemann und Ebert hingegen lebten nur am Rande meiner Welt. Ich kann dem Leser nichts von ihnen erzählen; obwohl es ihn sehr interessieren würde (weshalb eigentlich?)" (48).

10. "Doch gehörte das alles nicht zu meinem Jahr 1919" (53).

11. "Sie beherrschte meine Jahre 1923, 1924....Hitler und Ludendorff putschten; ich war in München....a schrieb mir, daß sie nie bei o bleiben würde, sondern zu mir zurückkäme, wenn ich mehr Geduld aufbrächte" (77).

12. "Es schmeichelte mir ganz enorm, daß ich für meine private Niederlage solch einen imponierenden Hintergrund erhielt" (121).

13. "Nur Menschen, nicht Ideen haben mich beeinflußt:...Philosophie war mir immer Menschen-, nicht Ideen-Geschichte" (25).

14. "Wer dieses Jahrhundert durchlebt hat, auch nur mit einem Mindestmaß von Gedächtnis—und ist kein Skeptiker geworden: dem ist nicht zu helfen" (221).

15. "Das lehrte mich die amerikanische Revolution, vorher die französische, nachher die russische....Wir sind gewöhnt, uns auf die Weltgeschichte zu verlassen. Auf sie ist kein Verlaß—aus dem einfachen Grunde, weil es sie nicht gibt" (376).

16. "...la douce France...meine ferne Geliebte..., bis ich mit ihr vom Jahre 1933 an als deutscher Emigrant....alltäglich zusammenleben mußte ...und da sah sie plötzlich ganz anders aus. Dann kam ich nach Amerika, in das Land der Jefferson-Reden, Walt Whitmanns und des deutschen Amerika-Enthusiasten, des Achtundvierzigers Carl Schurz—und wurde aufgeklärt, daß dies Land nicht ein Abbild der Preamble zur Declara-

tion of Independence ist...was nicht seine Schuld war, sondern meine Illusion" (43).

Chapter 5 Lion Feuchtwanger, *Unholdes Frankreich*

1. "Er hielt ...eine große Anklagerede. Er wies darauf hin, daß uns Frankreich ...Gastrecht versprochen hätte, ...daß er und...andere sich freiwillig zum französischen Militärdienst gemeldet hätten....Wir hätten alle bewiesen, daß wir bereit seien, im Kampf gegen Hitler unser Leben zu lassen. Aber...wir wollten nicht sterben als Opfer sinnloser französischer Bürokratie." Feuchtwanger, *Unholdes Frankreich*, 148-149.

2. "Die französischen Beamten waren bestechlich und versagten. Ihre Indolenz, ihre Käuflichkeit, ihre leere Routine war einer der Gründe, die zum Zusammenbruch Frankreichs führten" (69).

3. "Uns hatte man interniert...um der Bevölkerung ein Schauspiel zu geben. Man wollte die Aufmerksamkeit der Bevölkerung ablenken von denjenigen, welche in Wahrheit die Schuld trugen an den Fehlschlägen und an die man nicht herankonnte" (57).

4. "Wir hatten den Krieg mitmachen müssen, gebunden, gefangen, ohnmächtige Opfer einer unvernünftigen, wenn nicht böswilligen Militärclique" (116).

5. Similar to Feuchtwanger, Franz Schoenberner, who was also interned in Les Milles, claims that French indifference and incompetence were, in part, responsible for the collapse of France. *Innenansichten eines Aussenseiters*, 141.

6. "Dieser Krieg war unser Krieg. Hatten wir ihn verloren? Wir hatten ihn nicht verloren. Die französischen Faschisten hatten ihr Land unserm Feind ausgeliefert" (206). Feuchtwanger was not the only German writer subscribing to the view that the French themselves had delivered their country to the Germans.Cf.Hans Habe, *Ob Tausend fallen* and André Simone (Otto Katz), *J'accuse*. Fritjhof Trapp has challenged the factual accounts of the collapse and defeat of France in Habe's and Katz's texts. The latter, as mentioned earlier was, of course, a fictitious autobiography. Katz was not in France at the time of the invasion, but rather in the United States and Mexico. See Fritjhof Trapp "Fragwürdige Realismus-Behauptungen" *Exil. Forschung, Erkenntnisse, Ergebnisse* (Sonderband I), 114-126.

7. "Der Teufel in Frankreich war ein freundlicher, manierlicher Teufel. Das Teuflische seines Wesens offenbarte sich lediglich in seiner höflichen Gleichgültigkeit den Leiden anderer gegenüber, in seinem Je-m'en foutismus, in seiner Schlamperei, in seiner bürokratischen Langsamkeit....Daß er solcher Art war, war schlimmer, als wenn er grausam und böse gewesen wäre. Gegen Grausamkeit und Tücke hätte

man leichter angehen können als gegen Schematismus und Schlamperei" (114).

8. "all jenen Deutschen auszuliefern hätten, welche sie, die Nazi begehrten" (221).

9. "Nicht nur wollten die Franzosen von einer Mitarbeit von den deutschen Anti-faschisten nichts wissen, sie sperrten uns...ein" (27-28).

10. "Viele hatten in französischen Schlachten gefochten, einige im Kampf für die Sache Frankreichs einen Arm verloren oder ein Bein, fast alle besassen militärische Auszeichnungen. Selbst die Wachsoldaten waren erbittert, daß Frankreich diesen Männern die geleisteten Dienste nun so vergalt" (44).

11. Others interned in Les Milles corroborate Feuchtwanger's memories of the Legionaires. Cf.Schoenberner, *Innenansichten eines Aussenseiters* 140-141. Moreover, their own accounts support Feuchtwanger's condemnation of the pitiful state of hygiene at Les Milles. Cf. Alfred Kantorowicz, *Exil in Frankreich*, 110.

12. "Die mühselige Arbeit, die sinnlose Aufbuddelung des Grundes und die sinnlose Zuschüttung, war so recht ein Gleichnis unseres ganzen, sinnlosen, bedrohten Lebens in Les Milles" (125).

13. "eine einheitliche große Horde, abgerissen, verdreckt, verkommen" (104).

14. "Jetzt gerade jetzt, während du hier liegst, sitzen überall in der Welt Menschen, lesen deine Bücher über die Barbarei der Nazi, füllen ihr Herz an mit Grimm über diese Barbarei: du aber liegst hier, kläglich eingesperrt, menschenunwürdig, verdächtigt, ein Helfer jener Barbaren zu sein" (98-99)

15. "Noch jetzt, wenn ich daran denke, wie ich in dieser Schlange stand und wartete, überkommt mich ein Gefühl des Ekels, der Trauer, der Empörung, der äußersten Erniedrigung" (72).

16. "Es gab kein Wasser, man konnte sich vor dem Kot nicht retten und nicht vor den dicken Schwärmen von Fliegen" (71).

17. "In der Nacht hatte man den Zugang vom zweiten Stockwerk nach unten abgeschlossen....So verrichteten denn die oben ihre Notdurft, wo sie gerade waren, der Harn und Kot tropfte herunter zu uns in der Dunkelheit" (129)

18. "Ich hätte zwei Bücher mehr schreiben können, wenn ich die Zeit, die ich auf Ämtern und Kasernenhöfen, unnütz auf Unnützes wartend, zubringen mußte, auf meine Arbeit hätte verwenden dürfen" (67-68).

19. "...am schwersten erträglich im Lager war mir, daß man niemals mit sich allein sein konnte, daß immer, Tag und Nacht, bei jeder Verrichtung, beim Essen und beim Schlafen und bei der Entleerung, hundert Menschen um einen waren" (51)

20. "Ich werde mich darauf beschränken, darzustellen, was ich erlebt habe, so ehrlich, das heißt so subjektiv wie möglich und ohne den Anspruch, objektiv zu sein" (18).

21. Feuchtwanger's ruminations on subjective truth correspond closely to George Gusdorf's valorization of subjective truth in autobiography. "Conditions et limites de l'autobiographie" 118. Avrom Fleishman locates the philosophical origins of the valorization of subjective truth in the French tradition in Montaigne. Fleishman, *Figures of Autobiography*, 8.

22. Ich denke diese Willkür des Gedächtnisses ist ein Vorteil für den Schriftsteller. Sie nötigt ihn zu jener unbedingten Ehrlichkeit, welche die Voraussetzung aller Dichtung ist, sie nötigt ihn, nur solche Visionen zu geben, die wirklich seine Visionen sind....Ich muß infolge des Verlustes meiner Aufzeichungen ein Bild geben, nicht plumpe, fotografierte Wirklichkeit" (23).

Chapter 6 Hans Marchwitza, *In Amerika*

1. See Jack Zipes, "Die Freiheit trägt Handschellen im Land der Freiheit. Das Bild der Vereinigten Staaten von Amerika in der Literatur der DDR." Although Zipes does not specifically deal with Marchwitza's text, he provides an overview of other East German works dealing with the United States which, in part, mirror party ideology.

2. For a thorough discussion of America in German literature from the 17th to the second half of the 20th century see *Amerika in der deutschen Literatur* ed., Sigrid Bauschinger, Horst Denkler and Wilfried Malsch.

3. Marchwitza's highly negative memories and portrayal of the Statue of Liberty and the skyscrapers of Manhattan in the background correspond to the comments made by other exiled Communist writers. See Helmut Pfanner, *Exile in New York* 41-42. See further with regard to the exiles' literary reception and thematization of New York City, Michael Winkler, "Die Großstadt New York als Thema der deutschsprachigen Exilliteratur" *Deutschsprachige Exilliteratur seit 1933* Band 2, Teil 2; 1367-1384.

4. "Den Schmelztiegel hatte ich dieses New York schon einige Male nennen gehört; das sollte heißen: Hier, in dem Brodelkessel, wurden die aus aller Welt und in aller Not flüchtenden Hoffenden und von Erlösung Träumenden wie Plunder und rohes Material umgeschmolzen...um das zu werden, was New York brauchte: billige, willige Sklaven und Narren." Marchwitza, *In Amerika*, 439.

5. "Es sind Prüfungen, es ist Amerika...dieses eisige, herzlose Amerika" (390).

6. "Ich lag fast vierzehn Tage, von den Krämpfen völlig erschöpft, und hatte Zeit, über dieses Amerika nachzudenken, dessen unbegrenzte Möglichkeiten ich jetzt glaubte zur Genüge kennengelernt zu haben" (373).

7. "Als ich meine Hände in das heiße Sodawasser tauchte, schossen mir vor Schmerz die Tränen in die Augen. Beim Schrubben war mir zumute, als scheuerte ich mit schmerzgepeinigten Händen glühende Roste. Zum Glück fand ich einen alten Sachlappen, den ich mir unter die Knie legen konnte, in denen seit gestern brennende Dorne zu stecken schienen" (334).

8. "Ja, wir sind hier in Amerika....hier...mußt du selber die Maschine ersetzen" (344).

9. "... bogen und hoben und hämmerten wir...bis ich...manchmal ganz atemlos hinsank, um eine Minute lang auszuruhen" (ibid).

10. "Ja...das ist Amerika! Hier mußt du deine Gefühle draußen lassen und nur so ein Hebel oder Drehkran werden" (346).

11. "Ich dachte an den Tellerwäscher, der, wie diese Künstlerin, einmal gehofft hatte, hier in Amerika ein Mensch zu werden; mit ihren ersten Atemzügen im Lande der goldenen Freiheit begann ihnen der Betrug schon ihr Grab zu schaufeln" (353).

12. "Ich stand...inmitten der riesigen Betontürme...das Feldlager des Geldes—Börsenschlachten, Spekulation, Betrug, die Quelle des Irrsinns und ungezählter Morde und Selbstmorde" (305).

13. "daß ich für die deutschen Herren auch ein Neger gewesen und mit der gleichen Verachtung behandelt worden..." (396).

14. "Nicht diese Negermänner hatten die Siege in Nordafrika und Italien und auf den Inseln errungen. Amerika hatte sie errungen. Das Amerika der finsteren Zementtürme und der geschäftigen Bankbüros und der vollen Geldtresore" (413).

15. "Marschiere, schwarze, marschiere weiße Neger, das Vaterland des Unrechts, das Vaterland der Sklavenhalter muß verteidigt werden, es braucht Raum, Lebensraum..." (397).

Chapter 7 Fritz Kortner, *Aller Tage Abend*

1. Cf. Ernst Toller, *Eine Jugend in Deutschland*, 20-21. See further Peter Sloterdijk, *Literatur und Lebenserfahrung*, 135-136.

2. Cf. Egon Schwarz, *Keine Zeit für Eichendorff*, 18.

3. Ibid., 78, 127.

4. See "Aus den Papieren meiner Schwester.Vor der Deportation" Marcuse, *Mein zwanzigstes Jahrhundert* 328-347; Julius Hay, *Geboren 1900*, 40.

5. "Wir immer Lebensbedrohten...." Kortner, *Aller Tage Abend*, 98.

6. "Ich mag fünf oder sechsjährig gewesen sein, als ich eines Tages vor dem Geschäft meines Vaters...sitzend, vor mich hindämmerte. Zwei Spießgesellen erschienen mir... groß und gräßlich. Der eine Hühne beugte sich zu mir Schreckgelähmten nieder, seine Finger faßten nach meinen Haaren nah dem Ohr, wo sie am schmerzempfindlichsten sind, zwirbelten sie, zogen mich an ihnen in die Höhe, bis ich stand. Dann schlug der andere...dem Judenbuben ins Gesicht. Ich brüllte vor Schreck und Schmerz" (163).

7. Cf. Stephan Heym's recreation of his beating at the hands of anti-Semitic classmates in the Weimar Republic. *Nachruf*, 48.

8. "Und eines Tages als rote Rüben serviert wurden, fiel ich in Ohnmacht." *Aller Tage Abend*, 332.

9. "Mit dem Ponim können Sie nie den Melchtal spielen, mit dem Ponim können Sie überhaupt nicht zum Theater gehen. In einer Bank oder einem Geschäft spielt das keine Rolle" (41).

10. "Dem Meixner...verdanke ich nur wenig als Schauspieler, aber dafür das schwer zu überwindende Bewußtwerden meiner Häßlichkeit" (59).

11. See Hans Mayer, *Aussenseiter*, 311-458.

12. "...wieso ich als Jüngling...diese antijüdischen Pamphlete so unkritisch gelesen, ja ihnen zugestimmt hatte" (215).

13. "Ich stand bestürzt davor. Scheu und allein schlich ich ins Ghetto. Ich floß nicht über von Brüderliebe, wie ich es für meine Pflicht hielt. Ich scheute mich vor diesen mittelalterlichen Gestalten in langen Kaftans mit ihren...grotesk mich anmutenden gedrehten Locken an beiden Gesichtsseiten und langen Bärten" (111).

14. "Mein Assimilierungsprozeß hatte mich zu weit von ihnen entfernt. Ich war...dem Ghetto und seinen Gebräuchen weltenweit entrückt" (ibid).

15. "Was ich damals spielte war ich selber, ein jünger deutscher Jude, im Konflikt mit der Welt um sich herum" (218).

16. "Ich brannte darauf, ein Shylock zu sein, der, von der christlichen Umwelt unmenschlich behandelt, in Unmenschlichkeit ausartet. Ich ....wollte die Enthüllung des christlichen Hasses, die Aufzeigung einer morschen Moral" (242).

17. For a discussion of Kortner's career in the theatre, and the Jewish roles he played, see Matthias Brand, "Fritz Kortner in der Weimar Republik. Annäherungsversuche an die Entwicklung eines jüdischen Schauspielers", Diss; also by the same author "Aus der Vertreibung. Fritz Kortner im Exil (1933-1945)."

18. Ibid., 182.

19. "Mein Lebensvertrauen hängt an diesem Gerechtigkeitssymbol." Kortner, *Aller Tage Abend*, 281.

20. "...wir in unserer Jugend schon Bedrohten, wir zum Verfolgtsein auserwählten...wir immer Lebensbedrohten" (98).

Chapter 8 Toni Sender, *Autobiographie einer deutschen Rebellin*

1. Cf. Giesela Gabler-Brinker, Introduction to Toni Sender, *Autobiographie einer deutschen Rebellin*, 18.

2. See Sidonie Smith for a discussion of women writing autobiographical texts within traditional male narratives. "Self, Subject, and Reisistance: Marginalities and Twentieth-Century Autobiographical Practice" *Tulsa Studies in Women's Literature*, 1990: 11-24.

3. "Du (hast) fast nie geredet." Sender, *Autobiographie einer deutschen Rebellin*, 29.

4. "...die tristen Tage der Unterdrückung und des Gehorsams" (10).

5. "Wenige Lehrer hatten wahrscheinlich eine Vorstellung von der Heftigkeit der inneren Rebellion, die ich niederhielt" (32).

6. "Heute kann ich gestehen, daß ich keine Vorstellung davon hatte, zu welcher Laufbahn ich mich eigentlich entschloß. ...Das einzige, was für mich zählte, war, daß ich in zwei Jahren nicht mehr von meiner Familie abhängig sein würde" (34).

7. "wo meine Selbstständigkeit solche fesseln auferlegt worden waren" (47).

8. "zum ersten Mal in meinem Leben ...zu Hause!" (50).

9. "...die aktivste und wunderbarste Zeit meines Lebens" (ibid).

10. "Unter den ...Umständen, fürchtete ich, würde mich die Heirat in wirtschaftlichen und anderer Hinsicht von meinem Freund zu abhängig machen. Ich kannte mich gut genug, um zu wissen, daß es mein starkes Unabhängigkeitsgefühl zu sehr belasten und...die Harmonie zerstören würde, die bisher zwischen uns geherrscht hatte" (67).

11. "...ein Hagel von Schlägen. Mein Rücken schmerzte furchtbar....Dieser Abend ist Tausenden als Frankfurts Blutnacht in Erinnerung geblieben" (43).

12. "...von einem inneren Zwang getrieben, der stärker war als ich, und mußte den Weg weiter gehen" (28).

13. "ein entscheidender Augenblick in meinem Leben" (29).

14. "Ich schrieb. Ich verkündete den Erfolg der Revolution, die Gründung einer sozialen Republik. Ich teilte der Bevölkerung mit, daß Arbeiter- und Soldatenräte gebildet worden seien, die die oberste Autorität repräsentierten" (110).

15. "Nichts halb zu tun ist edler Geister Art. Diese Mahnung hat mich mein ganzes Leben lang begleitet und mich oft ermutigt und an den hohen Anspruch erinnert, mit dem ich angetreten war" (14).

16. "Schließlich konnte ich den gesundheitlichen Belastungen nicht standhalten. Ein hohes Fieber und eine schwere Grippe, die auch meine Lungen in Mitleidenschaft zog, warfen mich nieder" (123).

17. "die unser Wochenblatt von mir erwartete. Aber das Fieder hielt an" (123).

18. "In all diesen Tagen hatte ich nie die Kleider abgelegt, nicht geschlafen" (154).

19. "Meine Reaktion stand sofort fest. Unannehmbar! Ich hatte das Ringen der Arbeiter immer als einen Kampf um die Freiheit verstanden, nicht als die Unterwerfung von Fanatikern unter irgendein Oberkommando...in Moskau" (166).

20. "Ich hatte keine Zeit zur Erholung gehabt und bedurfte dieser dringend....Ich (mußte) von einem Bundesland zum anderen fahren, um gegen Redner aufzutreten, die unsere Partei spalten und sie in die kommunistischen Reihen und die Unterwerfung unter das Moskauer Zentralkommittee führen wollten....Ich war an vielen Orten erflogreich, wobei ich einmal dreieinhalb Stunden sprechen mußte....Es war eine bedeutsame Schlacht....und ich habe nie bereut, ihn....geführt zu haben" (167).

21. "Ich wurde immer schwächer und mußte... in ein Sanatorium. Mein Zustand besserte sich jedoch kaum" (172).

22. "Lungentuberkulose lautete die Diagnose des Arztes. Wieder war ich gezwungen, Krankenhaus und Sanatorium aufzusuchen-zuerst in Österreich, später in Deutschland" (175).

23. "Ich wurde an die Spitze der nationalen Liste gesetzt....Ich sollte dreizehn Jahre im Reichstag bleiben" (159).

24. "Eine Frau muß größere Anstrengungen unternehmen, muß mehr Tüchtigkeit beweisen als ein Mann, um als ebenbürtig anerkannt zu werden. Sobald ihre Fähigkeiten jedoch erkannt und anerkannt werden, spielt die Geschlechtszugehörigkeit keine Rolle mehr" (321).

25. "Meine Bemühungen waren darauf gerichtet, die Zollschranken durch gegenseitige Handelsverträge...abzubauen" (231).

26. "der einzige Wächter über die Interessen der Allgemeinheit und der Verbraucher zu sein" (239).

27. "Niemand war überrascht, als sich im Winter 1927 erneut die Tuberkulose meldete. Ein weiteres Mal fand ich mich auf dem Zauberberg in Davos" (234).

28. "Einige Vertreter des stärkeren Geschlechts fühlten sich bei Einbruch der Nacht ermüdet und außerstande, ihre Bemühungen fortzusetzen. Ich ermüdigte mich nie vor dem Ende der Sitzung — weil ich mir während meiner Tätigkeit im öffentlichen Leben immer Selbstdisziplin auferlegt hatte..." (239).

29. "Von der Vernünftigkeit meiner Position überzeugt, kämpfte ich mich beharrlich auf meinen Weg voran" (231).

30. "Ich hatte kaum zu sprechen begonnen, als ein Hagel von Zwischenrufen, Geschrei und Gelächter seitens der Nazis losprasselte. Ich konterte mit einem scharfen Angriff auf die Störenfriede. Nur in ihre Richtung gewandt, übte ich erbitterte Kritik an ihnen" (248).

31. "Seit den Septemberwahlen von 1930 hatte ich fast auf jeder meiner Versammlung mit den Nazis zu kämpfen" (250).

32. "Auf der Straße und in den Gastwirtschaften streuten sie nicht mehr und nicht weniger aus, als daß ich eine Prostituierte sei" (261).

33. "In Dresden gaben sie eine Zeitung mit dem Titel *Judenspiegel* heraus. Die ganze erste Seite nahm ein Bild von mir ein, und im Text darunter wurde angedeutet, daß man mich beseitigen solle" (270).

34. "Ich hatte ein hohes Fieber — ein Rückfall in meiner alten Krankheit" (276).

35. "Meine sozialistischen Genossen waren sehr überrascht, als ich ihnen... erklärte, daß sich einer der Männer mit Haushaltsfragen befassen müsse. Ich wollte das nicht tun" (133).

Chapter 9. Hilde Spiel, *Die hellen und die finsteren Zeiten 1911-1946*

1. "verdammte Hausfrauenexistenz." Spiel, *Die hellen und die finsteren Zeiten*, 240.

2. "ein starkes linguistisches Talent" (154).

3. "Unter Bomben entstanden, um unter Bomben geboren zu werden" (200).

4. "...das schlechte Gewissen plagt mich, weil ich Peter mit den Kindern...allein gelassen habe" (232).

5. "Das Wiedersehen mit den Kindern war beglückend, doch ich konnte nicht zur Ruhe kommen. Ich wollte gleich wieder ausschwärmen" (238).

6. "Fast zwei Monate habe ich schon meine Kinder allein gelassen" (247).

7. "Ich hatte es Brigid nennen wollen. Die folgenden Tage waren die schlimmsten meines Lebens" (195).

8. "Peter wollte von mir getröstet werden. Und mir war, als hätte ich im entscheidenden Augenblick versagt" (195).

9. "Peter, nicht zur Stelle, um zu helfen, zu trösten, 'es ist, als gäbe es ihn nicht,' erfuhr erst nach Wochen davon, ...Am zweiten August kam Peter zurück...geschwellt von Erfolgen und Aventüren jeglicher Art" (206).

10. "Peter hatte in seiner üblichen Nonchalance nicht ausreichend für uns gesorgt" (205).

11. "Ich mußte Geld borgen, um den Vater einäschern zu lassen" (206).

12. "Peter der Wandelbare" (216).

13. "In England kämpfe ich indessen nicht nur mit Kummer und Geldsorgen, sondern auch mit einer wachsenden inneren Unruhe, weil mir das Leben davonzulaufen ...droht" (ibid).

14. "Ich weinte vor Zorn" (238).

15. "Nie wieder eine solche Gewißheit, hier und nirgends anders beheimatet zu sein" (203).

16. "Ich glaube, ich könnte nirgendwo auch nur halb so glücklich und halbwegs so zufrieden sein, England paßt mir wie angegossen....Laß uns noch ein paar Jahre ausharren...Hier wird es uns gut gehen" (234).

17. "Da wußten wir, und gestanden's uns doch nicht ein: neun Jahre der Einfügung in die englische Welt waren vergeblich gewesen" (206).

18. "Aber wohin gehörten wir? Wer waren wir geblieben?, was geworden?" (207).

19. "...das Unerwartete, das Überraschende ereignete sich.Niemals zuvor oder danach sollten wir so eng mit den Briten verbunden sein wie in den nächsten drei Jahren, nie so sehr uns von ihnen angenommen fühlen wie auf eben jenem Festland, ...im Schutz ihrer Armee" (208).

20. "Sollte denn auch alles vergeblich gewesen sein—die längst hergestellte Vertrautheit mit dem Londoner Geistesleben, die engen Freund-schaften, der Umgang...mit so vielen Schriftstellern im und außerhalb des P.E.N., ...war meine Welt, eine andere hatte ich nicht mehr" (221).

21. "Ich bin sicher, daß ich um nichts in der Welt eine Wienerin sein möchte" (235).

22. "In den Entschluß, sich jetzt nicht an Ort und Stelle durchzubeißen und den Integrationsprozeß zu Ende zu führen, sondern—wenn auch diesmal für die Briten-nach Deutschland zu gehen, war die endgültige Rückkehr Jahrzehnte später schon eingebaut. Der Schicksalhafte Augenblick war versäumt. Denn nach unseren drei Jahren saß die gesamte heimgekehrte Kriegsgeneration ...der Engländer schon auf allen Stühlen. Wir aber waren von der deutschen Sprache, ja der deutschen Welt wieder vereinnahmt, ob wir's wollten oder nicht, und fanden in die britische nie mehr ganz zurück, obschon wir noch lange, lange weiter englisch schreiben und in unserem Londoner Vorort dahinvegetieren sollten" (234).

23. "Aber auch ich war Schuld. Ich wollte die Fesseln sprengen." (234).

Chapter 10 Franz Jung, *Der Torpedokäfer*

1. "Ich merkte sehr bald, daß ich ausgezogen war, nicht in die Gesellschaft hineinzuwachsen, sondern aus der Gesellschaft entfernt zu werden." Jung, *Der Torpedokäfer*, 38.

2. Jennifer Michaels characterizes Jung's self-representation in *Der Torpe-dokäfer* as the "compelling depiction of a tortured and lonely outsider" *Franz Jung. Expressionist, Dadaist, Revolutionary and Outsider* 163. Michaels also gives an overview of the very mixed reviews Jung's autobiography received upon its first publication in 1961; 158-163.

3. "einer der intelligentesten Menschen, die ich je getroffen habe, aber auch eine der unglücklichsten." George Grosz, *Ein kleines Ja und ein großes Nein*, 130.

4. See Horst Denkler's article "Der Fall Franz Jung: Beobachtungen zur Vorgeschichte der 'Neuen Sachlichkeit.'" *Die sogenannten zwanziger Jahre*, 75-107.

5. See Theo Meyer, "Revolte und Resignation: Eine Analyse von Franz Jungs *Torpedokäfer*" *Jahrbuch der deutschen Schillergesellschaft*, 23 (1979): 416-467.

6. Cf. Meyer, Ibid., 425.

7. "Ich habe den Ehrgeiz überwunden, als Schriftsteller anerkannt zu werden, als Geschäftsmann, als Liebhaber—und....selbst als anständiger Mensch." Jung, *Der Torpedokäfer*, 479.

8. "....wir haben uns bereits verdammt. Auch Sie, meine verehrten Leser werden dem nicht entgehen" (480).

9. "Nieder, mit dem Frieden!—und den Delirien einer kranken Gesellschaft, die parisitär ist ... (478).

10. "Die Geselllschaft, in die wir hineingeboren werden und in die wir gestellt sind, ist krank. Sie ist krank, weil die einzelnen, ...die zu dieser Gesellschaft zusammengeschlossen sind, krank sind, vergiftet, Träger der Anstiftung" (477).

11. "Ich hasse diese klassische Musik. Ich hasse Musik überhaupt" (42).

12. "Ich hasse meine Freunde. Sie sind diejenigen, die sich weigern werden, mir in die Hölle zu folgen" (479).

13. "In der Geschichte der erste Attentatsversuch gegen einen preußischen König und Kaiser....Ich bin sehr stolz darauf gewesen" (10).

14. "Ich habe meine Eltern nicht verstanden" (25).

15. "Ich weiß nur so viel, daß ich ständig abgeschoben wurde, beiseite gestellt" (27).

16. "Die Tragödie dieses Jahres traf mich mitten im Entwicklungsprozeß des Bewußtwerdens von Charakter und Persönlichkeit. Ich war damals vierzehn Jahre alt" (ibid).

17. "Der Onkel seinerseits schob mich ohne weitere Förmlichkeiten sogleich nach Leipzig ab" (37).

18. "In dieser Gesellschaft fühlte ich mich wohl" (49).

19. "Ich glaube, ich hatte damals die ernste Absicht, den Beruf eines Zuhälters zu wählen" (52).

20. "Niemals ist jemand gekommen und hat zu mir gesprochen. Niemals" (66).

21. "Soviel ich weiß, verlangt man von einem Schriftsteller, daß er das, was er schreibt, durcharbeitet und feilt, auswägt und den Leser oder Hörer hineinzuziehen bestrebt ist. Ich habe das nicht getan. Ich stoße eher den Leser ab. Mir fehlt von vornherein die Distanz" (67).

22. "Ich bin nicht gewillt gewesen, um meine Anerkennung als Schriftsteller...ernsthaft zu kämpfen; jedenfalls schien das einigen Verlegern

so und Leuten aus dem Literaturbetrieb, die bereit gewesen wären zu helfen" (302).

23. "das große Erlebnis meines Lebens" (156).

24. "Das war es, was ich gesucht habe und wozu ich seit meiner Kindheit ausgezogen bin: die Heimat, die Menschenheimat" (156).

25. "Ich bin mir vorgekommen wie der Neuling im Boxingring, der plötzlich in eine Serie von Schlägen hineingelaufen ist und sich am Boden wiederfindet. Er steht wieder auf und versucht sich zu erinnern, woher und wie es zu den Schlägen gekommen ist" (236).

26. "Praktisch war ich ein Außenseiter, ein störendes Element...auch mit einem messianischen Gedanken, der beim Neuaufbau einer Gesellschaft immer ein Störenfried und Schädling bleiben wird" (290).

27. The figure who also had an important influence on Jung was the psychoanalyst Otto Groß. See Arnold Imhof, *Franz Jung. Leben, Werk, Wirkung*, 62 ff.

28. Jung became the posthumous editor of Furhmann's *Grundformen des Lebens. Biologisch-philosophische Werke*. See Michaels op. cit., 167-170.

29. "Ich leide darunter, daß ich oder der einzelne bestimmt ist zu leiden, er existiert ungeschützt, mit einem völligen Mangel an Selbstverteidigung....Der einzelne bleibt allein" (390-391).

30. "Es ist die biologische Eigenschaft des Käfers, daß er das Ziel anfliegt und stürzt....Ich habe den Flug unzähliger Male in mir selbst erlebt. ...Das Ende ist immer das gleiche gewesen. Anprall, Sturz, Kriechen am Boden, sich zurückbewegen zum Startplatz-mit Mühe und jedesmal mit größeren Anstrengungen. Die Wand, gegen die der Käfer anfliegt, ist solide gebaut. Generationen von Menschheit stehen dahinter" (406)

31. "ob der einzelne in der Gesellschaft aufgenommen und betreut wird oder ausgestoßen" (333).

Chapter 11 Robert Neumann's *Ein leichtes Leben*

1. "Hitler hat mich meiner Rechte als Staatsbürger und meines Besitzes beraubt." Sender, *Autobiographie einer deutschen Rebellin*, 282.

2. "Wie schäbig, erbärmlich, ist es, hier wegzulaufen....fliehen zu müssen....abermals fliehen." Döblin, *Schicksalsreise*, 114.

3. "Dante genügte es, von Florenz nach Pisa zu gehen, der von Hitler Verfolgte wurde durch die Kontinente gejagt." Hilde Domin, *Von der der Natur nicht vorgesehen*, 144.

4. "Denn losgelöst von allen Wurzeln und selbst von der Erde, die diese Wurzeln nährte – das bin ich wahrhaftig wie selten einer in den Zeiten." Zweig, *Die Welt von Gestern*, 7.

5. "Von all meiner Vergangenheit habe ich also nichts mit mir, als was ich hinter der Stirne trage" (11).

6. "Wieder war es Abschied. Ich dachte an die vielen Abschiede, die ich in den fünf Jahren bereits hinter mir hatte. Nach jedem war etwas zerbrochen, ein jeder hinterließ eine Enttäuschung." Marchwitza, *In Frankreich*, 8.

7. "Das alles trug viel zu meiner Desillusionierung bei, zu dem Gefühl der Auflösung, ja die Zertrümmerung einer Existenzform durchzuleben." Schwarz, *Keine Zeit für Eichendorff*, 3.

8. "In der Emigration ist jeder Freund, jeder Bekannte wertvoller Besitz, ein Stück Vergangenheit." Castonier, *Stürmisch bis Heiter*, 306.

9. "Dies Erlebnisbuch soll eine Brücke bauen, das heute mit dem gestern verbindet....Eine Brücke über den Riß der Zeit hinweg." Pauli, *Der Riß der Zeit geht durch mein Herz*, 9.

10. "...beide gingen an einer Krankheit zugrunde: dem Mangel an Zukunft." Marcuse, *Mein zwanzigstes Jahrhundert*, 225.

11. "Alles, was ich seit der Vertreibung unternommen hatte, mußte unter dem Zeichen des Provisoriums, des ständig bevorstehenden Abbrechens stattfinden....Diese Lebensform hatte mir als eine Entschuldigung gedient für alles Halbfertige, alles Mißglückte, sowohl in der Arbeit als auch in menschlichen Beziehungen." Weiss, *Fluchtpunkt*, 251.

12. References to Dilthey's importance for the theory of classical autobiography begin with his son in-law, Georg Misch, *Geschichte der Autobiographie* I, 8. See further, Roy Pascal, *Design and Truth in Autobiography*, 177-8; James Olney, "Autobiography and the Cultural Moment" *Autobiography: Essays Theoretical and Critical*, 8; Janet Varner Gunn, *Autobiography: Torward a Poetics of Experience*, 7-8; Katherine Goodman. *Disclosures: Women's Autobiography in Germany between 1790 and 1914*, vi-vii.

13. See Ingrid Aichinger, *Künstlerische Selbstdarstellung*, 34.

14. "Zu bedenken, obgleich es ein unfruchtbarer Gedanke ist...ob man bei diesem endgültig letzten Versuch, sein Leben aufzuschreiben, nicht doch besser sehr viel früher eingesetzt hätte? Meine Ahnen waren – dann meine Eltern, dann ich selbst, ab, c, d,? Aber ich habe ein tiefes Mißtrauen gegen die Kontinuität der Zeit....Ich habe ein tiefes Mißtrauen, bezüglich unserer Position in ihr." Neumann, *Ein leichtes Leben*, 43.

15. "... aus verwelktem Leben...." (15).

16. "Abgebrochen....Wo, wann wie beginnen?" (18).

17. "Mir ist eingefallen, ganz ohne Zusammenhang" (458).

18. "...es findet sich kein direkter Zusammenhang" (481).

19. "All das schiebt sich durcheinander, es ergeben sich Probleme der Chronologie" (301).

20. "Ich weiß nicht, wie das alles zusammenhing" (348).

21. "Nein, es war nicht ganz einfach" (505).

22. "Und nun stand ich da...Rip van Winkel, jemand hatte mir die besten dreißig Jahre meines Lebens gestohlen" (505).

23. "Aber wessen Autobiographie gibt von wem ein Bild?" (422).

24. "Eine Fotographie aus jener Zeit präsentiert mich als liebliches, weiches Kind, mit einem unschuldigen halboffenen Kindermund. Lange, sorgfältig gebürstete Haare umrahmen ein ernstes, rührendes Gesicht" (300).

25. "Um seine Lippen spielt ein idiotisches Lächeln" (323).

26. "Mit dem Mann, der dies niederschreibt, hat er—vielleicht bis auf die spärlich gewordenen Spuren jenes idiotischen Lächelns—so viel zu tun wie der Mann im Mond" (323).

27. "Ich habe mich immer wieder von Menschen getrennt" (497).

28. "Mein Leben mit A zerbrach...wegen...Linda" (314).

29. "Und nicht einmal von B habe ich etwas gesagt" (46).

30. "die Linie von Mutter zu Tochter durch diese Jahrhunderte" (192)

31. "Jene Urgroßmutters-mutter, die in ihrem glücklichen Leben nur einmal vergewaltigt und davon ein einzigesmal schwanger ward. Sie war die Tochter einer, die wurde in einem einzigen Kriegsjahr siebzehnmal vergewaltigt. Wessen Tochter also? Wessen Sohn bin ich selbst? Wer meine Vettern? Welcher preußischer Junker, welcher dunkle Araber, welcher sowjetische Kommissar? Mein Blut, meine Begierde, Angst, Leidenschaft—wessen Angst? Wessen Blut?" (192).

32. "Das verblüffende ist die Beharrlichkeit, mit der das Haus durch sechs Jahrhunderte zu dieser Funktion zurückkehrte" (258).

33. "Alarmierend...., daß man trotz aller gegenteiligen Bemühungen sich selbst mit geringerer Härte anfaßt als alle andere" (308).

Chapter 12 Ludwig Marcuse, *Auf dem Weg zu einer Autobiographie*

1. Marcuse's defense of the alleged obscene and pornorgraphic in literature is found in Marcuse's *Obzön. Geschichte einer Entrüstung.*

2. "Ich finde die Quelle seiner wesentlichen Mängel im Mangel am Mut."
   Marcuse, *Mein zwanzigstes Jahrhundert*, 386.

3. "Ich hab's nicht gewagt, die Geschichte meines Körpers in meine
   Geschichte hineinzuschreiben" (387).

4. "Ein Leben ist nicht zulänglich geschildert, in welchem die Natur-und
   Sozialgeschichte der zur Seele gehörigen Haare und Ohren und Beine
   und Hoden und Gerüche und Gesten nicht deutlich gemacht wird..."
   (388).

5. Helmut Heißenbüttel "Anmerkungen zu einer Literatur der Selbstentblößer", 86.

6. "Daß der Einzelne aus einer Seele plus einem Kerker aus Fleisch
   besteht, geht nicht allein auf christliche Verketzerung zurück: Platon
   sah im Leib ein Gefängnis der Seele....und nach ihm sahen alle
   philosophierenden Seelen, daß der so sichtbare Leib recht lästig werden kann." Marcuse, *Nachruf*, 104.

7. "kennte er die Geschichte seines Körpers genauer" (137).

Chapter 13 Walter Mehring, *Die verlorene Bibliothek*

1. See p. 137 of this study.

2. Cf., Erich Kleinschmidt, "Schreiben und Leben. Zur Ästhetik des Autobiographischen in der deutschen Exilliteratur" *Exilforschung* Vol.2; 36.

3. See page 5 of this study.

4. "Buch über Bücher...." Mehring, *Die verlorene Bibliothek*, 289.

5. "...es lag mir nicht so sehr an den Büchern im einzelnen, sondern an
   jener historisch, ästhetisch, philosophisch einmaligen Konfigurationen,
   wie sie sich in der Bibliothek meines Vaters, in seinem speziellen
   Horoskop des XIX Jahrhunderts eingestellt hatte" (19).

6. "Doch nie hatte mein Vater....ein Musterschüler der kritischen Ver-
   nunft—unter den Bänden seiner Bibliothek die Toxine, die Keimträger
   okkulter Epidemien gearwöhnt" (20).

7. "gefährlichsten Komponente der Seele: Genie und Irrsinn" (21).

8. "Ich war in meines Vaters Bibliothek allzu streng beaufsichtigt zu der ethisch unpraktischen Illusion verzogen worden, Kulturkatastrophen könnten durch die Radikalkur eines bewaffneten Generalstreiks... verhütet werden...wie eine venerische Ansteckung durch eine rechtzeitige medizinische Behandlung" (151).

9. "die Teufelsbuhlschaft zwischen Hexen und Ketzern, und die Succubengeilheit des Weibes, die ... das Foltern zu einer praktischen Wissenschaft ausgebildet hatten" (60).

10. "gar nichts anders als die ewige Unruhe der Romantik....die tiefste Wirklichkeit des selbst, des 'Elan-vital' Philosophen Henri Bergson. In Italien wurde sie als Fascismo von dem Quattrocento-Epigonen Gabriele d'Anunzio, von dem Futuristen Marinetti zur Form vom einem 'Popolo'–Journalisten, Benito Mussolini, als staatliche Normaluhr gleichgeschaltet" (195).

11. "...die Symbole, mit denen die Wirklichkeit uns entsetzt" (169).

12. "Selbst zum Bombenattentat—bekannte sich auer mein Vater....aber wenn, dann ganz und gar als zu einem Notwehrakt des Individuums gegen den Staat" (28).

13. "Eine hinschwindende Oberschicht wurde von dem Rudelblick, von dem 'Vorwärts-und-Nieder-mit...Geheuel' von den Indianertänzen um das Individuum am Marterpfahl hypnotisiert....und die nüchternsten Dialektiker nachtwandelten mondsüchtig am Dachfirst der Kollektiv-Logik" (159).

14. "demolierte die fortschritthinderlichen Hotels, deckte die Dächer des Privatlebens ab, stieß die Cafehäuser um, zerwalzte die Wälder, Wiesen und Almen; die Heiligen Stätten der schöpferischen Individualität....Vor allem ist er hinter Büchern drein, die von Lebensgenuß und Einzelleid handeln" (264).

15. "In Deinem Zeitalter hat man aus den Schicksalen Bücher gemacht—in dem unsern sind die Bücher unser Verhängnis geworden" (186).

Conclusion

1. Cf. Hugo Dittberner, *Heinrich Mann: Eine kritische Einführung in die Forschung* 57. Mann's interpretation of history reflects, apart from the influence of Hegel, also that of Nietzsche and Michelet. See Klaus Schröter, *Heinrich Mann. Untertan-Zeitalter-Wirkung*, 47-48.

2. "Wir fühlten uns ...wie Vieh, das sich unter dem gehobenen Beil des Henkers ängstigt." Marcuse, *Mein zwanzigstes Jahrhundert*, 162.

3. "Wir, die wir von diesem Mann geflohen waren, fürchteten uns." Castonier, *Stürmisch bis heiter*, 304.

4. "Wir die Emigranten waren froh, daß die Zeit des sinnlosen Nachgebens dem Barbarentum gegenüber endlich vorbei war" (301).

5. See Wolfgang Emmerich, "Die Literatur des anti-faschistischen Deutschlands" *Die deutsche Literatur im Dritten Reich*, 441. Emmerich's remarks concentrate on the reports published in the early years of the Third Reich, while Helmut Peitsch discuses the autobiographical reports of former concentration inmates published in the Western Zones of Germany immediately after the war. *Deutschlands Gedächtnis an seine dunkelste Zeit* 101-102; 147-150.

6. "daß es auch hier Antisemitisimus gab, daß unsere Gewißheit, all dem faschistischen Unwesen für immer entronnen zu sein auf einer bloßen Illusion ruhte....Hitlers Gift, der moderne politische Antisemitismus war auch hierher gedrungen und ich empfand es als tiefe Enttäuschung, als mir nach unserer Ankunft aus einem Lautsprecher eine judenfeindliche Propagandarede entgegenplärrte" (78).

7. "Ich trocknete sie, und ... (sie) wurde in einem Kuvert aufbewahrt mit der Aufschrift:Haut von Lion." Marta Feuchtwanger, *Nur eine Frau*, 38. A close reading of her text also reveals a subtext in which she presents the story of her own singularity and individuality in contradistinction to that of Lion Feuchtwanger's.

8. See Sylvia M. Patsch, "Und alles ist hier fremd." *Deutsche Literatur von Frauen*, 305.

9. "Die Diktatur des Proletariats." Sender, "Die Frauen und das Rätesystem", reprinted in the appendix to Giesela Brinker-Gabler; ed., Toni Sender, *Autobiographie einer deutschen Rebellin*, 289.

10. See note 8 to introduction.

11. "Was bleibt unsereins im Exil übrig als von Erinnerungen zu leben und Memoiren zu schreiben." Quoted in Weiskopf, *Unter fremden Himmeln*, 96.

12. Cf. Rainer Zimmer, "Zur Autobiographik des Exils 1933-1945", 221, 227.

Works Cited

Autobiographical Texts of the Exiles

Castonier, Elisabeth, *Stürmisch bis heiter. Memoiren einer Aussenseiterin*. München: Nymphenburger Verlagsbuchhandlung, 1964.

Döblin, Alfred, *Autobiographische Schriften und letzte Aufzeichnungen* ed. Edgar Pässler. Olten: Walter Verlag, 1980.

____. *Schicksalsreise. Bericht und Bekenntnis*. Frankfurt: Carolus Druckerei, 1949;

Domin, Hilde, *Von der Natur nicht vorgesehen. Autobiographisches*. München: Piper, 1974.

Feuchtwanger, Lion, *Unholdes Frankreich*. Mexico D.F.; El Libro Libre, 1942.

____. *The Devil in France. My Encounter with Him in the Summer of 1940* Trans. Elisabeth Abbot. New York: Viking, 1941.

____. *Der Teufel in Frankreich. Erlebnisse*. Rudolstadt: Greifenverlag, 1954.

Feuchtwanger, Marta, *Nur eine Frau*. München: Albert Langen, 1983.

Frank, Leonhard, *Links wo das Herz ist*. München: Nymphenburger Verlag, 1952.

Frei, Bruno, *Der Papiersäbel. Autobiographie*. Frankfurt: S. Fischer, 1972.

Grosz, George, *Ein kleines Ja und ein großes Nein, Sein Leben von ihm selbst erzählt*. 1955. Reinbeck: Rowohlt, 1983.

Gumpert, Martin, *Hölle im Paradies. Selbstdarstellung eines Arztes.* Stockholm: Bermann-Fischer, 1939.

Haas, Willy, *Die literarische Welt.* München: P. List, 1957.

Habe, Hans, *Ob Tausend fallen.* London: Hamilton, 1943.

Hay, Julius, *Geboren 1900. Aufzeichnungen eines Revolutionärs.* München: Heyne, 1980.

Hermlin, Stephan, *Abendlicht.* Berlin: Verlag Klaus Wagenbach, 1980.

Heym, Stephan, *Nachruf.* Frankfurt: Fischer, 1990.

Hildesheimer, Wolfgang, *Zeiten in Cornwall.* Frankfurt: Suhrkamp, 1973.

Hiller, Kurt, *Eros.* Reinbeck: Rowohlt, 1973.

Jung, Franz, *Der Torpedokäfer.* 1961. Neuwied: Luchterhand, 1972.

Kantorowicz, *Deutsches Tagebuch.* München: Kindler, 1959.

____. *Exil in Frankreich.* Bremen: Schünemann Universitätsverlag, 1971.

Koestler, Arthur, *Ein spanisches Testament. Aufzeichnungen aus dem Bürgerkrieg.* Zürich: Europa Verlag, 1938.

____. *Dialogue with Death.* Trans. Trevor and Phyllis Blewitt. New York. Macmillan, 1942.

____. *Darkness at Noon.* New York: Macmillan, 1941.

____. *Sonnenfinsternis.* London: Hamilton, 1946.

____. *The Gladiators.* New York: Macmillan, 1939.

____. *Die Gladiatoren.* Hamburg: A. Springer, 1948.

____. *The Invisible Writing. Second Volume of an Autobiography.* New York: Macmillan, 1954.

____. *Die Geheimschrift*. München: Desch, 1954.

Kortner, Fritz, *Aller Tage Abend*. 1959. München: DTV, 1969.

Mann, Klaus, *The Turning Point*. New York: L.B. Fischer, 1942.

____. *Der Wendepunkt. Ein Lebensbericht*. Frankfurt: G.B. Fischer, 1960.

Mann, Heinrich, *Ein Zeitalter wird besichtigt*. 1945. Berlin: Classen, 1974.

Marchwitza, Hans, *In Amerika*. Berlin: Verlag Tribüne, 1961.

____. *In Frankreich*. Potsdam: Rütten & Loening, 1949.

____. *In Frankreich. In Amerika*. Berlin: Aufbau Verlag, 1971.

Marcuse, Ludwig, *Mein zwanzigtes Jahrhundert*. München: Paul List Verlag, 1960.

____. *Nachruf auf Ludwig Marcuse*. Stuttgart: List, 1969.

____. *Obzön. Geschichte einer Entrüstung*. München: P. List, 1962.

____. *Obscene. History of an Indignation*. Trans. Karen Gershon. London: MacGibbon and Kee, 1965.

Mehring, Walter, *The Lost Library. Autobiography of a Culture*. Trans. Richard and Clara Winston. New York: The Bobbs-Merrill Co., 1951.

____. *Die verlorene Bibliothek. Autobiographie einer Kultur*. Hamburg: Rowohlt, 1952.

Neumann, Robert, *Ein leichtes Leben. Bericht über mich selbst und die Zeitgenossen*. Wien: Verlag Kurt Desch, 1963.

Pauli, Herta, *Der Riß der Zeit geht durch mein Herz. Ein Erlebnisbuch*. Wien: Zsolnay, 1970.

Regler, Gustav, *The Great Crusade*. New York: Longmans, 1940.

_____. *Juanita. Ein Roman aus dem spanischen Bürgerkrieg.* Frankfurt: Büchergilde Gutenberg, 1986.

_____. *Das Ohr des Malchus. Eine Lebensgeschichte.* Köln: Kiepenheuer & Witsch, 1958.

_____. *The Owl of Minerva. The Autobiography of Gustav Regler.* Trans. Norman Denny. New York: Farrar Straus and Cudahy, 1960.

Sahl, Hans, *Exil im Exil.* Darmstadt: Luchterhand, 1990.

_____. *Memoiren eines Moralisten. Erinnerungen I.* Zürich: Amann Verlag, 1983.

Schwarz, Egon, *Keine Zeit für Eichendorff. Chronik unfreiwilliger Wanderjahre.* Königstein: Athenäum, 1979.

Schoenberner, Franz, *Confessions of a European Intellectual.* New York: Macmillan, 1946.

_____. *Bekenntnisse eines europäischen Intellektuellen I.* Trans. Elisabeth Stark. München: Kreisselmeier, 1964.

_____. *The Inside Story of an Outsider.* New York: The Macmillan. 1949.

_____. *Innenansichten eines Aussenseiters II.* Munich: Kreisselmeier, 1965.

Sender, Toni, *Autobiography of a German Rebel.* New York: Vanguard Press, 1939.

_____. *Autobiographie einer deutschen Rebellin.* With an introduction by Giesela Brinker-Gabler. Trans. Brigitte Stein. Frankfurt: Fischer, 1981.

Simone, André (Otto Katz), *J'accuse! The Men who betrayed France.* New York: The Dial Press, 1940.

Sperber, Manès, *Die Vergebliche Warnung: All das Vergangene.* Wien: Europa, 1975.

____. *Die Wasserträger Gottes: All das Vergangene.* Wien: Europa Verlag, 1974.

____. *Wie eine Träne im Ozean.* Köln: Kiepenheuer, Witsch, 1961.

Spiel, Hilde, *Die hellen und die finsteren Zeiten. Erinnerungen 1911-1946.* Munich: List Verlag, 1989.

____. *Welche Welt ist meine Welt? Erinnerungen 1946-1989.* List Verlag, 1990.

Toller, Ernst, *Eine Jugend in Deutschland.* Amsterdam, Querido, 1933.

____. *I was a German.* Trans. Edward Crankshaw. New York: Morrow, 1934.

Weiss, Peter, *Fluchtpunkt.* Frankfurt: Suhrkamp, 1962.

Zweig, Stefan, *Die Welt von Gestern.* Stockholm: Bermann Fischer, 1944.

____. *The World of Yesterday.* New York: Viking Press, 1951.

Zuckmayer, Carl, *Als wär's ein Stück von mir.* Frankfurt. Fischer, 1966.

Secondary Works Cited

Aichinger, Ingrid, *Künstlerische Selbstdarstellung: Goethes 'Dichtung und Wahrheit' und die Autobiographie der Folgezeit.* Bern: Peter Lang, 1977.

Bollenbeck, Georg, *Zur Theorie und Geschichte der frühen Arbeiterlebenserinnerungen.* Kronberg: Scriptor, 1976.

Brand, Matthias, "Aus der Zeit der Vertreibung: Fritz Kortner im Exil 1933-1947" Fritz Kortner, *Theaterstücke Donauwellen und Nacht und Nebel* ed. Matthias Brand. Köln: Prometheus Verlag, 1981. 182-200.

_____. "Fritz Kortner in der Weimarer Republik. Annäherungsversuche an die Entwicklung eines jüdischen Schauspielers" Diss. Berlin 1969.

Bruss, Elizabeth, *Autobiographical Acts: The Changing Situation of a Literary Genre.* Baltimore: Johns Hopkins University Press, 1976.

Caute, David, *The Fellow Travellers. A Postscript to the Enlightenment.* New York: Macmilian, 1973.

Critchfield, Richard, "Arthur Koestler's Ein spanisches Testament: Crisis and Autobiography" in: *German and International Perspectives on the Spanish Civil War: The Aesthetics of Partisanship* Eds. Luis Costa, Richard Critchfield, Joe Golsan and Wulf Koepke. Columbia: Camden House, 1992. 68-76.

_____. "Heinrich Mann's View of History and the Allied Leaders in *Ein Zeitalter wird besichtigt*: Visions of Utopia" in: *Der Zweite Weltkrieg und die Exilanten. Eine literarische Antwort* Ed. Helmut Pfanner. Bonn: Bouvier, 1991. 221-228.

____. "Einige Überlegungen zur Problematik der Exilautobiographik" in: *Exilforschung. Ein Internationales Jahrbuch* 2 (1984): 41-55.

____. "Autobiographie als Geschichtsdeutung" *Deutsch-sprachige Exilliteratur*. Eds. Wulf Koepke and Michael Winkler. Bonn: Bouvier, 1984. 228-241.

Crossman, Richard ed. *The God that Failed*. New York: Harper, 1949.

De Mann, Paul. "Autobiography as De-facement," *Modern Language Notes* 94 (1979): 919-930.

Denkler, Horst, "Der Fall Franz Jung: Beobachtungen zur Vorgeschichte der 'Neuen Sachlichkeit'" in: *Die sogenannten Zwanziger Jahre*. Eds. Reinhold Grimm and Jost Hermand. Berlin: Gehlen, 1970. 75-107.

Dilthey, Wilhelm, *Gesammelte Schriften VII*. Göttingen: Vandenhoeck & Ruprecht, 1973.

Dittberner, Hugo, *Heinrich Mann, Eine kritische Einführung in die Forschung*. Frankfurt am Main: Athenäum Verlag, 1974.

Eaken, Paul John, *Fictions in Autobiography: Studies in the Art of Self-Invention*. Princeton: Princeton University Press, 1985.

____. "Narrative and Chronology as Structures of Reference and the New Model Autobiographer" in: *Studies in Autobiography*. Ed. James Olney. New York: Oxford University Press, 1988. 32-41.

Emmerich, Wolfgang, *Proletarische Lebensläufe* 1848-1914 Vol.I. Reinbeck: Rowohlt, 1974.

____. *Proletarische Lebensläufe* 1914-1945 Vol. II. Reinbeck: Rowohlt, 1975.

____. "Die Literatur des antifaschistischen Widerstandes in Deutschland" in: *Die deutsche Literatur im Dritten Reich.* Eds. Horst Denkler and Karl Prümm. Stuttgart:Reclam, 1976. 427-458.

Fleishman, Avrom, *Figures of Autobiography.* Berkeley: University of California Press, 1983.

Frühwald, Wolfgang, "Exil als Ausbruchsversuch. Ernst Tollers Autobiographie" *Die deutsche Exilliteratur 1933-1945* ed. Manfred Durzak. Stuttgart: Reclam, 1973. 489-498.

Funk, Mueller-Wolfgang, "Das Exil ist eine Krankheit: Autobiographien als ein Mittel sich zu behaupten" in: *Merkur* 414 (1982): 1231-1236.

Frieden, Sandra, *Autobiography: Self into Form: German Language Autobiographical Writings of the 1970's.* Bern: Lang, 1983.

Goodman, Katherine, *Dis/Closures: Women's Autobiography in Germany Between 1790 and 1914.* Bern: Peter Lang, 1986.

Graber, Heinz, "Politisches Postulat und autobiographischer Bericht. Zu einigen im Exil entstandenen Werken Alfred Döblins" in: *Die deutsche Exilliteratur 1933-1945.* Ed. Manfred Durzak. Stuttgart: Reclam, 1973. 418-429

Gunn, Varner, Janet, *Autobiography: Towards a Poetics of Experience.* Philadelphia: University of Philadelphia Press, 1982.

Gusdorf, George, "Conditions et limites de l'autobiographique." in: *Formen der Selbstdarstellung: Analekten zu einer Geschichte des literarischen Selbstportraits.* Eds. Günter Reichenkron and Erich Hasse. Berlin: Duncker & Humblot, 1956.

____. "Conditions and Limits of Autobiography" Trans. James Olney, *Autobiography. Essays, Theroetical and Critical* Ed. J. Olney. Princeton: Princeton University Press, 1980. 28-48.

Heissenbüttel, Helmut, "Anmerkungen zu einer Literatur der Selbstentblößer" in: Heissenbüttel *Zur Tradition der Moderne: Aufsätze und Anmerkungen 1964-1971.* Neuwied: Luchterhand, 1972. 80-94.

Herder, Johann Gottfried, *Sämtliche Werke* ed. Bernhard Suphan, Reprint: Hildesheim: Olm, 1967.

Imhof, Arnold, *Franz Jung, Leben, Werk, Wirkung.* Bonn: Bouvier Verlag, 1974.

Koepke, Wulf, "Die Flucht durch Frankreich:Die zweite Erfahrung der Heimatlosigkeit in Berichten der Emigranten aus dem Jahre 1940" in: *Exilforschung: Ein Internationales Jahrbuch* 4 (1986): 229-242.

Jauß, Hans Robert, "Literaturgeschichte als Provokation der Literaturwissenschaft" in: Jauß, *Literaturgeschichte als Provokation.* Frankfurt: Suhrkamp, 1970.

Kleinschmidt, Erich "Schreiben und Leben: Zur Ästhetik des Autobiographischen in der deutschen Exilliteratur" in: *Exilforschung: Ein Internationales Jahrbuch* 2 (1984):24-40.

Krause, Rolf D. "KZ-Wirklichkeit und KZ-Darstellung zwischen 1935 und 1940. Zu den autobiographischen KZ-Berichten der Exilliteratur" *Exil. Forschung, Erkenntnisse, Ergebnisse* Sonderband I (1987):176-188.

Lejeune, Philippe, *Le pacte autobiographique.* Paris: Editions du Seuil, 1975.

____. *On Autobiography* Ed. Paul John Eakin; Trans., Katherine Leary. Minneapolis, University of Minnesota Press, 1989.

Loesberg, Johanthan, *Fictions of Consciousness.* New Brunswick: Rutgers University Press, 1986.

Mayer, Hans, *Aussenseiter.* Frankfurt: Suhrkamp, 1975.

Meyer, Theo, "Revolte und Resignation: Eine Analyse von Franz Jungs *Torpedokäfer*" in: *Jahrbuch der deutschen Schillergesellschaft*, 23 (1979): 416-467.

Misch, Georg, *Geschichte der Autobiographie*. 4 vols. Bern: Francke, 1949-50 (vol. I); Frankfurt: G. Schulte-Bulmke, 1955-1969 (vols. 2-4).

____. *A History of Autobiography in Antiquity*. Trans. E.W. Dickles. 2 vols. Cambridge: Harvard, 1951.

Michaels, Jennifer, *Franz Jung. Expressionist, Dadaist, Revolutionary and Outsider*. New York: Peter Lang, 1989.

Moore, Erna M., "Exil in Hollywood: Leben und Haltung deutscher Exilautoren nach ihren autobiographischen Berichten" in: *Deutsche Exilliteratur seit 1933 I. Kalifornien*. Eds. John M. Spalek and Joseph Strelka. Bern: Franck, 1976. 21-39.

Müller, Klaus-Detlef, *Autobiographie und Roman*. Tübingen: Niemeyer, 1976.

Münchow, Ursula, *Frühe deutsche Arbeiterautobiographien*. Berlin: Akademie, 1973.

Neumann, Bernd, *Identität und Rollenzwang: Zur Theorie der Autobiographie*. Frankfurt: Athenäum, 1970.

Niggl, Günter, *Geschichte der deutschen Autobiographie im 18. Jahrhundert: Theoretische Grundlegung und literarische Entfaltung*. Stuttgart: Metzlar, 1977.

____. Ed. *Die Autobiographie: Zu Form und Geschichte einer literarischen Gattung*. Darmstadt: Wissenschaftliche Buchgesellschaft, 1989.

Olney, James, *Metaphors of the Self: The Meaning of Autobiography* Princeton: Princeton University Press, 1972.

____. *Autobiography: Essays: Theoretical and Critical*. Princeton: Princeton Univ. Press, 1980.

Pascal, Roy, *Design and Truth in Autobiography*. Cambridge: Harvard University Press, 1960.

Patsch, Sylvia M., "Und alles ist hier fremd" in: *Deutsche Literatur von Frauen. Zweiter Band 19. Und 20. Jahrhundert*. Ed. Gisela Brinker-Gabler. München: Beck, 1988. 304-317.

Paulsen, Wolfgang. *Das Ich im Spiegel der Sprache: Autobiographisches Schreiben in der deutschen Literatur des 20. Jahrhunderts*. Tübingen: Max Niemeyer Verlag, 1991.

Peitsch, Helmut, *Deutschlands Gedächtnis an seine dunkelste Zeit: Zu Funktion der Autobiographik in den Westzonen Deutschlands und in den Westsektoren von Berlin 1945 bis 1949*. Berlin: Sigma Rainer Bohn Verlag, 1990.

Petto, Hans Dieter, "Auf der Suche nach dem Land der Politik. *Juanita*, Gustav Regler's anderer Spanienkriegsroman" in: *Gustav Regler-Dokumente und Analysen* Eds. Uwe Grund, Ralph Schock and Günter Scholdt. Saarbrücken: Saarbrücker Druckerei und Verlag, 1985.

Pike, David, *German Writers in Soviet Exile, 1933-1945*. Chapel Hill: University of North Carolina Press, 1982.

Pfanner, Helmut F. *Exile in New York: German and Austrian Writers after 1933*. Detroit: Wayne State University Press, 1983.

Prangel, Matthias, *Alfred Döblin*. Stuttgart: Metzler, 1973.

Prater, D.A., *European of Yesterday. A Biography of Stephan Zweig*. Oxford: 1972.

Radkau, Joachim, "Der Historiker, die Erinnerung und Das Exil. Hallgartens Odyssee und Kuczynskis Prädestination" in: *Exilforschung: Ein Internationales Jahrbuch* 2 (1984): 86-103.

Schock, Ralph, *Gustav Regler-Literatur und Politik 1933-1940*. Frankfurt: Fischer Verlag, 1984.

Schröter, Klaus, *Heinrich Mann. Untertan, Zeitalter, Wirkung: Drei Aufsätze.* Metzler: Stuttgart, 1971.

Schuster, Ingrid, and Ingrid Bode, eds. *Alfred Döblin im Spiegel der zeitgenösischen Kritik.* Bern: Francke Verlag, 1973.

Schwab, Sylvia. *Autobiographik und Lebenserfahrung. Versuch einer Typologie deutschsprachiger autobiographischer Schriften zwischen 1965 und 1975.* Würzburg: Epistemata, 1981.

Schwarz, Egon, "Was ist und zu welchem Ende studieren wir Exilliteratur" in: *Exil und innere Emigration II: Internationale Tagung in St Louis.* Eds. Peter Uwe Hohendahl and Egon Schwarz. Frankfurt: Suhrkamp, 1973. 15.

Shumaker, Wayne, *English Autobiography.* Berkeley, University of California Press, 1954.

Sloterdijk, Peter, *Literatur und Lebenserfahrung: Autobiographien der Zwanziger Jahre.* München: Hanser Verlag, 1978.

Smith, Sidonie, "Self, Subject, and Resistance: Marginalities and Twentieth-Century Autobiographical Practice" in: *Tulsa Studies in Women's Literature* 9, 1 (1990): 11-24.

Sprinker, Michael, "Fictions of Self: The End of Autobiography" in: *Autobiography: Essays Theoretical and Critical.* Ed. James Olney. Princeton: Princeton University Press, 1980. 321-342.

Trapp, Frithjof, "Fragwürdige 'Realismus'-Behauptungen- Hans Habe: *Ob Tausend fallen* und André Simone: *J'Accuse!*" in: *Exil, Forschung, Erkenntnisse, Ergebnisse* Sonderband I (1987): 114-126.

Walter, Hans Albert, "Die Grenzen des Erinnerungsvermögens: Kritische Anmerkungen zur Autobiographie von Julius Hay" in: *Frankfurter Hefte 2* (1972): 107-116.

Wegner, Matthias *Exil und Literatur: Deutsche Schriftsteller im Ausland 1933-1945.* Frankfurt am Main: Athenäum Verlag, 1967.

Weintraub, Karl Joachim, "Autobiography and Historical Consciousness" in: *Critical Inquiry* I (1975): 821-48.

____. *The Value of the Individual: Self and Circumstance in Autobiography*. Chicago: The University of Chicago Press, 1978.

Weiskopf, F. C. *Unter fremden Himmeln*. Berlin: Dietz Verlag, 1948.

Werner, Renate, *Heinrich Mann. Texte zu seiner Wirkungsgeschichte in Deutschland*. Tübingen: Max Niemeyer Verlag, 1977.

Winkler, Michael, "Die Großstadt New York als Thema der deutschsprachigen Exilliteratur" in: *Deutschsprachige Exilliteratur seit 1933 2*. New York Eds. John M. Spalek and Joseph Strelka. Bern: Francke Verlag, 1989. 1367-1384.

Zimmer Rainer, "Zur Autobiographik des Exils 1933-1945" in: *Faschismuskritik und Deutschlandbild im Exilroman* (Special Issue of *Literatur im historischen Prozess. Neue Folge* 2 (1981): 214-227.

Zipes, Jack, "Die Freiheit trägt Handschellen im Land der Freiheit. Das Bild der Vereinigten Staaten von Amerika in der Literatur der DDR" in: *Amerika in der deutschen Literatur*. Eds. Sigrid Bauschinger, Horst Denkler and Wilfried Malsch. Stuttgart: Reclam, 1975.

Index

Literature and the Sciences of Man

This interdisciplinary series is predicated on the conviction that the inevitable development toward increasing specialization requires as its correlative a movement toward integration between the humanities, social sciences, and natural sciences. Titles in the series will deal with "multidisciplinary" figures, as well as with movements affecting a variety of disciplines. The series editor will also consider manuscripts dealing with methods and strategies in the domains of aesthetic creation, the arts of criticism, and scientific exploration.

Please direct all inquiries to the series editor.

Peter Heller
Dept. of Modern Languages &
    Literatures
SUNY-Buffalo
Buffalo, NY 14260